T0272555

THE MAN WHO PUT A CURSE ON
MUHAMMAD
ALI

THE MAN WHO PUT A CURSE ON

MUHAMMAD
ALI

The Downright Crazy Story of
Richard Dunn's World Title Challenge

Norman Giller

A Norman Giller Books Publication
In association with Pitch Publishing

Pitch Publishing
9 Donnington Park,
85 Birdham Road,
Chichester,
West Sussex,
PO20 7AJ
www.pitchpublishing.co.uk
info@pitchpublishing.co.uk

www.normangillerbooks.com

A CIP catalogue record is available for this book
from the British Library.

ISBN 978 1 80150 542 0

Typesetting and origination by Pitch Publishing
Printed and bound in Great Britain by TJ Books, Padstow

Contents

Previous Pitch Publishing books by Norman Giller:

The Ali Files

My 70 Years of Spurs

Sir Geoff Hurst's Eighty At Eighty
(nominated for Sports Book of the Year)

The One and Only Jimmy Greaves (the official biography)

In loving memory of Muhammad Ali.

Simply The Greatest

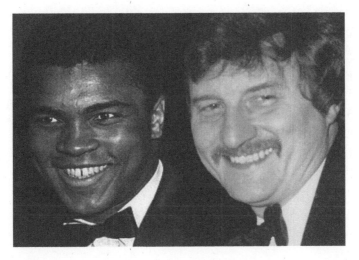

Muhammad Ali with author Norman Giller in the 1970s

Author's note

I was hoping to write this extraordinary story in harness with its main character, Richard Dunn. Unfortunately, this loveable British bulldog of a man became a victim of the dreaded ex-sportsman's curse of dementia and was left with only hazy memories of the crazy night he gave Muhammad Ali a fight and a fright. Every word I write on the following pages is true, with occasionally a name, location or incident timing changed to protect the innocent – and me from any legal comebacks. I was a disbelieving eyewitness of everything that happened in my role as publicist for the fight that was not supposed to happen, and I am the only person who could possibly have written this version of events. Fasten your seat belt. You are in for a shocking ride and – occasionally – a laugh or three. I promise you could not make it up.

PART ONE

Seconds Out

Setting the scene for Muhammad Ali's strangest and funniest fight night

THIS WAS the fight that was never supposed to happen; Muhammad Ali against Yorkshireman Richard Dunn for the heavyweight championship of the world at the Olympiahalle in Munich on 24 May 1976. I was ringside in my role as publicist for a contest that bankrupted the promoters and lost more money than almost any other title fight in history.

Six weeks earlier, British and Commonwealth champion Dunn had battled with much-hailed German kaiser Bernd August at London's Royal Albert Hall for the European title vacated by Joe Bugner. The winner would meet Muhammad Ali for the world crown.

The Ali fight had already been confirmed for Munich, with the undefeated August expected with some certainty to be the opponent. There was no way, so the experts predicted, that he could lose to Dunn, whose career had largely followed the Baron de Coubertin principle of the importance of taking part rather than winning.

Dunn threw a spanner – no, a pickaxe – in the works with a two-fisted, swinging attack that staggered and then separated the shambling August from his senses, the referee having to rescue the 6ft 7in Berlin giant as he stumbled semi-conscious around the ring in the third round. Poor old August was one of life's losers – just a few years later he was killed in Australia when his motorbike collided with a kangaroo.

As the referee raised Dunn's hand in astonishing, unexpected victory, Philadelphian entrepreneur Butch Lewis jumped into the ring with a jewelled crown meant for August and jammed it lop-sided on the head of 'King Richard', who looked suitably bemused.

A handsome but very short black man, Lewis had to reach up to perform the coronation and did not quite get the placement right, leaving Richard looking a complete plonker. The renowned BBC commentator Harry Carpenter was overheard to say off camera, 'What a circus. Send in the clowns ... don't bother, they're here,' from Stephen Sondheim's *A Little Night Music* which had just arrived in town from Broadway.

Lewis had the fairly odd fashion quirkiness of wearing a flashy, silk floral tie knotted around his neck, but no shirt. The fight had been staged during the IRA bombing campaign on London and the ringside security men were frightened, uh, shirtless as Lewis dived into the ring.

None of us involved in the show at the British end had any idea that he planned the crowning of the new champion. It might just about have worked if August had won, but it was condemned by the British press as a gimmick too far. Richard summed it up beautifully in true Yorkshire fashion when he told me privately, "Ell's bells, I felt a reet pillock.'

I was at the Albert Hall as publicist for joint promoters Mike Barrett and Mickey Duff, and as I watched the pantomime of the crowning ceremony I got a strange premonition that I was about to become involved in one of the weirdest fight promotions in history. The feeling was akin to sensing that the inmates were taking over the asylum and I had been cast as one of the patients.

A beaming Butch Lewis, blissfully unaware of the panic his crowning stunt had caused, told the American

TV audience: 'Richard Dunn has now become Emperor of Europe. The question is, can he take the world crown from mighty Muhammad Ali? Watch this TV space.'

I was later given the crown that had been plonked on Richard's head and was instructed to return it to the Palladium theatre props department. The panto season was still with us.

It was a $3m final punch from Dunn that wrecked the unfortunate August. That is how much it cost the German promoters when they stubbornly and stupidly went ahead and put on Ali's title defence in an after-midnight fight in Munich. Translated into 2023 money that was around $23m down the drain.

I try to hide it on my CV that I worked on this event as a publicist for a promotion that haemorrhaged money like no other before or since. The German public had no enthusiasm for watching a virtually unknown Brit, even though the legend that was Ali provided the opposition. To be honest, Richard was hardly a household name in his own country until his shock victory over August suddenly catapulted him into the headlines.

On fight night the ultra-modern, 14,000-seat Olympiahalle, sitting at the heart of the sprawling 1972 Olympic Park, was barely half full, populated by hundreds of British boxing fans who had flown in from Yorkshire and the thousands of American soldiers enjoying a complimentary night out. They were given fistfuls of free tickets by Ali as he toured the local United States Army military camps drumming up last-minute publicity for a contest that carried little interest for German boxing fans.

The fight should instantly have been switched to the UK the moment that sandy-haired southpaw Dunn detonated his right fist on August's lantern jaw, but the German promoters were locked into the ego trip of being involved in a Muhammad Ali world title defence.

An Ali fight was not just a boxing match, it was an occasion. The German boxing fraternity, however, was too sceptical to fall for handing over their hard-earned Deutsche Marks to watch a Brit they had never heard of challenge the most famous boxer in history.

The local promotion syndicate ignored the sage, cut-your-losses advice of their vastly experienced American partner Bob Arum and insisted on keeping the fight in Munich. This meant putting up thousands of dollars in purse guarantees, local taxes, stadium rent and hotel bills.

They had been spoilt and sated with full houses for the Olympics and football World Cup finals in the previous four years, and were convinced the legend of Muhammad Ali would guarantee *penner auf den sitzen* – bums on seats. Ja, to watch Bernd August against Ali. But Richard Dunn? Neun, neun, neun; that could have been an emergency call for their bank accounts.

Ali was into the wind-down period of his career after his sensational 'Rumble in the Jungle' and 'Thrilla in Manila' championship victories over George Foreman and Joe Frazier. He had given many of the millions of dollars he had earned to charities, ex-wives and his Islam-inspired management team; now he was just fighting for the cash to look after himself and his family in retirement.

He was on a guaranteed $1.65m to defend his title against modern Cinderella Man Dunn, whose $100,000 (£52,000) purse was almost as much as he had earned in all his previous 43 fights, nine of which he had lost.

A scaffolder when he was not scrapping, 31-year-old Richard was like a man who had won the lottery but would have to go to hell and back to collect his prize money.

Luckily he had a head for heights, because he was about to be lifted to the heavens and then dumped unceremoniously on the canvas in the ring in Munich. But not before landing some telling blows on the man who justifiably described himself as The Greatest.

So that's the scene for what has to go down in the history books as Muhammad Ali's strangest and funniest fight night. Now I invite you to take a ringside seat for the championship contest and a build-up that could have come out of the script of a *Carry On* film. You could not make it up.

Seconds out; here comes our hidden 'hero', an English gentleman – I almost said con artist – known as Romark.

Round One

Of Romark, Crystal Palace and Elvis

RONALD MARKHAM, stage name Romark, a self-styled hypnotist, mentalist, illusionist and mind-reader, sat confidently behind the wheel of his canary-yellow Renault. The black velvet blindfold covering his eyes had been checked by a neutral judge to ensure he could not see through it. He was now ready to drive solo and sightless through the busy Ilford highway on the edge of Greater London, using just his instincts and impulses. What could possibly go wrong?

A pack of paparazzi photographers and reporters prepared to follow him as he slipped the car into first gear and set off on his unseeing way along Ilford Broadway. To make other motorists more considerate of him he was steering a vehicle with a huge learner-driver logo on the roof.

He had gone all of 20 yards on the perilous journey when he smashed into the back of a parked vehicle, which just happened to be a police transit van, commonly known back then as a Black Maria.

I promise it is close to verbatim when I quote the startled policeman sitting at the wheel of his vehicle as saying, 'Hello, hello, hello, what's going on here then?'

He got out of his van and walked with some indignation towards the driver of the car that had whacked into him, and he was fairly surprised to find him sitting at the steering wheel wearing a blindfold. During a brief interview, he elicited from the flustered Romark that he was a hypnotist and mind-reader who was trying to prove he could drive blind towards London. 'If you're a mind reader,' opined the veteran and cynical police sergeant, 'you will know what I am about to say next; you're nicked.'

Romark was not prepared to admit guilt. 'But,' he protested, 'my thought processes did not allow for an illegally parked vehicle. You should not have been there. Ilford Broadway is a public thoroughfare that should be kept clear of any obstructions.' As we will learn later in our story, he always had an answer or an excuse for everything.

This was the same Romark who had just the previous year – so he claimed – given Crystal Palace Football Club a promotion push by hypnotising their key players. When manager Malcolm Allison refused to pay him a previously agreed fee, Romark put a curse on Palace that he insisted cost them victory in an FA Cup semi-final against Southampton on 3 April 1976.

I called on Southampton manager Lawrie McMenemy for his take on the myth and he told me, 'It's true that this strange man offered to help us beat Palace. I thought I would listen to him just in case, so to speak, he had a trick up his sleeve. He tried to convince me he had psychic powers by getting one of our apprentices to levitate in my office. It was mind-blowing stuff but our trainer George Horsfall, who had been born in India, performed the same feat and said he had learned it from one of those guys who do the Indian rope trick. Romark later claimed credit for our win over Palace, but I prefer to think our players and my tactics had more to do with it!'

Now here he was back in the spotlight with the car stunt that went hilariously wrong. He made nationwide news as the motorist who tried to drive blind across London. I stored all this away in the recesses of my publicist's mind, wondering how I could use his gift for generating headlines.

Meantime, I had been given the job of publicising the upcoming Muhammad Ali–Richard Dunn world heavyweight title fight in Munich. I was hired by the millionaire businessman Jarvis Astaire, who had launched a trend-setting closed-circuit theatre company called ViewSport.

Jarvis and I were fellow East Enders and had known each other since I served my writing apprenticeship on the trade paper *Boxing News* in the 1950s. I was freelancing after ten years as chief football reporter for the *Daily Express*, which in those days sold 4.2 million copies a day. Back then, Jarvis was a shadowy figure who got a full-page apology from *Boxing News* after it suggested that he was the mystery 'Mr X' running a syndicate with the aim of unseating Jack Solomons as the tsar of British boxing promoters.

By the 1970s, imaginative impresario Jarvis had become one of the wealthiest men in the country (and pretty rich in the town, too) after marrying into the fabulously wealthy Oppenheim family. He was a visionary who had his fingers in many promotional pies and was at various times a property developer, movie star Dustin Hoffman's manager, theatre and film producer, Lester Piggott's racehorse owner, deputy chairman of Wembley, chairman of the Greyhound Racing Association, the hidden force behind professional wrestling promotions, a generous charity fund-raiser and a close friend and confidant of Tony Blair. The epitome of a 'Champagne Socialist'.

I remember him telling me how he had once tried to bring Elvis Presley to Europe for his only concert outside the United States. 'I negotiated with his manager, "Colonel" Tom Parker,' he said, 'and offered £2m for a one-off concert at Wembley Stadium. That was a colossal amount at the time. The Colonel responded, "That's very generous of you, Jarvis. Now then, what about the boy?"'

His ViewSport company set the pioneering pace for what was later to become satellite television, and my brief was to place stories in newspapers to help put bums on seats at British cinemas for a contest that was not scheduled to start until 3am GMT. We publicised it as an 'after-midnight' fight, knowing that the main event was delayed until three o'clock – four o'clock in Munich – to allow for it to be shown 'live' by NBC at peak time in the United States.

With the Munich box office as lively as a cemetery, it was television and closed-circuit TV money that was keeping the fight alive. There were just five weeks to go to the show when I was appointed as ViewSport's PR, and ticket sales could be counted on the fingers of a one-armed bandit.

Royal Albert Hall promoter Mike Barrett told me from behind his trademark heavy-framed, horn-rimmed spectacles, 'If they'd let us switch it to England we could guarantee a full house at either Headingley [the Test cricket ground] or Elland Road [Leeds United's football stadium]. Richard has become the hero of Yorkshire. But the Germans are going to go ahead with the fight in Munich where it'll be a hard sell, even with Muhammad Ali in the opposite corner. Let's not forget he stank the place out in his last fight.'

A sluggish, weary-looking Ali had laboured to a points victory over Jimmy Young in Maryland on 30 April 1976, weighing a career-heaviest 230lb (16st 4lb) and for one of the few times in his career he was booed and jeered by many in the crowd.

Wearing my publicist's hat, I latched on to the plodding Ali performance against Young and started spreading the word that he was ready for the taking. Did I believe it? Of course not, because I was an Aliphile who truly believed his mantra, 'I am The Greatest.'

I had become a spin doctor, trying to pump life into my patient that was the Ali–Dunn fight. It was in critical condition. There were worrying reports coming from Munich that the German promoters were squabbling among themselves as to whether they should go ahead with the show and this negative news was leaking into the British newspapers. I was a poacher turned gamekeeper and found myself lying to old colleagues as I assured them the fight was going ahead. Not my finest hour. I had sold my soul.

In desperation, I tried to get my old friend Henry Cooper on to the Dunn bandwagon, but he was not going to play the lying game. 'He is not in the same class as Ali,' said the man whose 'ammer of a left hook once put the then Cassius Clay on to the seat of his pants. That was back in 1963. The great man was now 13 years older, slower and showing the signs of his ring wars. But he was still the legend that was Muhammad Ali.

The best I could get Henry to agree to was to release a story quoting him as saying, 'Dunn has got a puncher's chance.' Privately, he told me that Ali would 'eat him alive'.

My strength as a publicist was that I was on friendly conversation terms with all the major Fleet Street sportswriters, many of whom I had shared press boxes, trips to overseas events and adventures and escapades with during the previous ten years in my life as a reporter. But I don't think anything had quite prepared me for the challenge of trying to attract people to watch a fight that should never have been.

* * *

The first thing I did to generate publicity was prepare a Richard Dunn fact file that I faxed to every major newspaper and magazine sports desk in the land.

Yes, that's right, faxed. This was long before Tim Berners-Lee invented the World Wide Web in 1989. Just as an aside so that you appreciate the era in which we were operating, in the very week that the fight was staged Queen Elizabeth II sent the first electronic message from a head of state. I recall that my first email account with BT was normangiller@telecomgold.com. Trouble is very few people were registered, so I was talking to myself. But back to the story of the build-up to the world championship contest.

This is how my faxed fact file read, typed on my faithful old Remington portable typewriter that had accompanied me to sports events around the world:

RICHARD DUNN FACT FILE
Submitted by Norman Giller
For VIEWSPORT

Born Halifax, West Riding of Yorkshire
Birthdate: 19 January 1945
Grew up in Leeds, now lives in Bradford.
British, European and Commonwealth heavyweight champion 6ft 4in tall, weighs around 15st.
Southpaw stance. Likes to lead with his right jab from long range and follow up with left hooks that carry knockout power.

Known to his building site workmates as Dick, or Dickie.

Fights: 42; wins 33 (16 inside the distance).

Married to Janet, daughter of his trainer Jimmy 'Pop' Devanney. Three children, Rocky, Karen and Gillian. Ten siblings.

Was semi-pro rugby league player before switching full time to boxing in 1969.

Continues to work as a part-time scaffolder.

Managed since 1974 by Leicester-based George Biddles.

Turned his career round after three successive stoppage defeats in 1974, when he contemplated retirement.

Is a soldier in the Territorial Army, attached to the 4th Battalion Parachute Regiment, rank sergeant. He has made 67 parachute drops.

Note to sports editor: I shall be in Munich with Richard and his entourage two weeks before the fight and will be filing fee-free stories every day. ViewSport will be screening live coverage of the fight and all the supporting contests to selected theatres and cinemas, with ringside commentary by Reg Gutteridge.

Free tickets available for competition prizes. Please contact me for full details.

* * *

Now all we needed was a fight.

Round Two

This Is Your Life, New York New York

FOLLOWING RICHARD Dunn's startling European title victory over Bernd August, I helped scriptwriters Tom Brennand and Roy Bottomley put together a hurried *This Is Your Life* tribute from Eamonn Andrews to the affable Yorkshireman. It was to lead to me writing for the show for 14 years, first for Eamonn and then his successor Michael Aspel.

Our star guest with a contribution from the States was Muhammad Ali, who had great fun teasing his challenger about Yorkshire puddings and his parachuting with the Territorial Army. 'You've got one more landing to make,' said Ali, pretend-snarling into the camera, 'and it will be face first on the canvas when I annihilate you in Munich.'

Only Ali would turn a *This Is Your Life* programme to his psychological advantage. Richard's only retort was to laugh along with the rest of us. He was being thoroughly entertained, forgetting that behind the jokes Ali was being deadly serious. And he was coming to get the Brit!

Richard had made 67 jumps with his parachute regiment and was renowned for his feats of strength, including getting a gold medal award for once carrying the trunk of a tree on his own on an assault course after his three team-mates had dropped out exhausted. He was still first across the finish line on his own, carrying the huge tree across his back. Richard was one of the most determined characters I ever encountered.

When he first met Janet he was torn between making boxing or rugby league his profession, and it was his wife-to-be who persuaded him that he was better equipped to make a living with gloves on rather than boots. 'I owe everything I am to Jan,' he told me. 'To be honest I was a bit of a tosser who liked to scrap on the cobbles until she tamed me and taught me how to control my strength and my temper. Without her, I think I might have finished up behind bars or somewhere on a slab in a mortuary.' As I quote Richard here he comes across as somebody easy to understand, but you need to imagine him talking in pure Yorkshire without use of the definite article and with aitches consigned to the bin. And for 'was' he would invariably substitute 'were', and when he was discussing his boxing career he would switch to the royal 'we' as if he had somebody doing the fighting with him.

It's fair to say that Richard was starstruck by Ali, and he rolled sideways in his chair laughing during his *This Is Your Life* tribute as he watched the world champion threatening him on the screen. 'You've gotta love the man,' he said, which were not quite the hateful words we needed to drum up publicity for their title fight.

Richard and his loving wife Janet were then whisked off to the United States for a whirlwind tour of New York and the NBC studios. Their feet had not touched the ground since his victory over August, and the pair were later to recall it as the most exciting time of their lives. Everybody who met the couple in the US fell in love with them, Janet in particular because of the way she sheltered and protected her husband from hangers-on and time-wasters.

She had met Richard through her father Jimmy Devanney, who trained him as well as his two professional boxing sons, Jim junior and Lawrence. It was part of the Devanney family legend that Janet was the one with the specialist knowledge who was as handy with her fists as any of them.

Richard and Janet – 'my lass, the best thing that ever happened to me' – had worked on an Ali-style poem on the flight to the States in their first-class VIP seats:

Muhammad Ali, I think yer a square
I'm going to retire you to a rocking chair
At 34, you ain't so young
Yer going to get whupped by me, Richard Dunn

It was not quite Byron or Wordsworth, and lost a lot of its quality in its delivery because to American ears Bradford's Richard Dunn was just about unintelligible. Eeh bah gum, he just might as well have been speaking in a foreign tongue. What was that George Bernard Shaw once said about the US and Britain being two countries divided by a common language?

When Richard came face-to-face with Ali at a televised press conference organised by NBC, all his rehearsed insult lines were wasted because the American audience, including the champion, did not understand much of what he said in his heavy Yorkshire accent.

His most aggressive line after Ali had hit him with a volley of verbal abuse was, 'Every donkey likes to hear itself bray.'

This was rather lost on American ears and Ali had to ask him to repeat it, which meant it had lost its sting – or, rather, kick – by the time it had been translated.

Even the Louisville Lip was lost for words and took to appearing to try to throttle Richard until dragged off by his ham-acting henchmen. He had been referring to his opponent as 'Frankenstein's Monster' and pointed to the small, bespectacled Jimmy Devanney and identified him as Igor, which amused rather than aggravated the Dunn camp. Instead of getting riled on his father-in-law's behalf it was all Richard could do to stop himself laughing out loud.

Richard later told me, 'As Ali left the stage, he leant over to me, squeezed my arm and whispered, "Let's go and make some mon-eeey!" How could I even pretend to dislike the man? I'd hero-worshipped him for years. He was my idol and I was going to share a ring with him. Pinch me, I must be dreaming.'

I watched the press conference on a BBC feed at its White City studios with Mike Barrett, who summed it up when he told me, 'That was good entertainment, but won't sell a single ticket.'

Selling tickets – bums on seats – had suddenly become my priority. From wordsmith to salesman, my conscience in cold storage.

I sat down and drew up a list of ideas, and uppermost in my mind was an eccentric, possibly certifiable hypnotist called Romark.

But first, I had to have a one-on-one session with Richard Dunn. What made the big man tick?

The American press had already nicknamed him Joe Palooka, after the newspaper cartoon-strip hero of the 1940s. It was my job to try to prove he was not Europe's paper champion.

Round Three

Torture at the old farmhouse gym

RICHARD DUNN was showing me around an old farmhouse barn on the edge of Bradford that had been converted into a boxing gymnasium, including an 18ft square ring with ropes slackened to imitate the 'Rumble in the Jungle' setting. 'I've sweated my bollocks off here,' he said, wincing at memories of painful exercises and private battles with the heavy punchbag that hung down from a gnarled oak beam, like a body swinging on the gallows. Alongside the bag, nailed to the wall, was a wooden toilet seat and glued to it was a fading photograph of Joe Bugner. 'No man in't world has worked harder than me to be where I am today, with the British, Commonwealth and European titles to my name. Mind you, we've had some hard knocks on the way, haven't we Pop?'

Father-in-law Jim Devanney, Richard's trainer, mentor and the man Muhammad Ali had dubbed Igor, nodded agreement. 'Eeh, you're reet there, lad,' he said in pure Yorkshire. 'But as Sophocles said, "There's no success without hardship."' Richard laughed and beamed as he saw my double take while I tried to get my head round 'Igor' quoting Greek philosopher Sophocles.

'Jim, I call him Pop, is one of the best-read men you'll ever meet,' he said proudly, as if introducing me to his college professor. 'He's a quiet bloke who never boasts, but could lose most people in a general knowledge quiz. Always comes out with amazing facts. He's a walking encyclopaedia.'

The trainer, in his late 50s, wearing thick-lensed glasses signalling short-sightedness to go with his short stature, dark greying hair, centre-parted, brushed back 1950s-style, looked shyly down at his feet. 'I'm a bookaholic,' he admitted. 'T'missus is always threatening to burn my books. Our house is packed solid with them. I had no education to speak of and am always looking to improve my knowledge. It were Einstein who said, "Wisdom is not a product of schooling but of the lifelong attempt to acquire it."'

Sensing that I could quickly be out of my depth, I decided to bring us back to the less challenging topic of boxing. I pointed to the toilet-seat insult of Joe Bugner, who had relinquished the titles that Richard now held. 'Guess you don't rate Bugner,' I said, knowing that was a massive understatement.

'Can't stand t'bloke,' Richard said, with the sort of naked hatred I wanted him to show in the build-up to the fight for the world title. 'When he got his chance against Ali last year he just took t'money and ran; or rather danced. Didn't try an inch to beat Ali and then went for an hour-long swim in his hotel pool. Just fought to survive. It were disgraceful.'

'We call him the dancing statue,' Jimmy added. 'How could he challenge for t'world heavyweight championship and not give his all?'

'I'm ready to die, if I have to,' Richard said with a sudden intensity that startled me. 'They're going to have to carry me out of there on my shield. This is a chance of a lifetime and I'm determined to take it. I've jumped out of airplanes into t'unknown, run through tackles on t'rugby field, smashed down opponents much bigger than me in t'ring. That's the fighting spirit I'm taking to Munich. Ali fought like a shadow of himself against Jimmy Young and if he comes in against me in that condition he'll be in trouble.'

I wasn't going to be the one to interrupt Richard in this fighting mood and point out that in 1974 Jimmy Young had stopped him in eight rounds. Perhaps it was the Yorkshire air that had given him sudden bravado, and as he walked me across the surrounding picturesque moors from the gymnasium I began to get vibes that he really believed he could conquer The Greatest.

'I've been given this chance in a million to win t'greatest prize in sport,' Richard said as we sat down in a nearby cafe drinking tea from chipped mugs and looking out at views that could have come right out of an episode of *Last of the Summer Wine*. All it needed was Norah Batty to come by in her wrinkled stockings.

'I'd loved to have had t'fight here in Yorkshire,' Richard said, with almost a dream look on his wide, pugilistic face which had scar tissue over both eyes and a flattened nose as evidence of wars in the ring and battles on the rugby league field. 'Can you imagine t'support with a packed Headingley crowd behind me? But it's pointless thinking that way. The fight is in Munich and I'm getting myself in't frame of mind that I'm going to war.'

The publicist in me nearly cheered as I made notes for an article I would be releasing through the Press Association, the agency that had a telex machine in every major newspaper editorial office in the land. If only Richard had come out with this fighting talk in his recent press conference with Ali, when he came across as subdued and too respectful.

There were now barely three weeks to go to the fight in Munich and the news on the ticket-selling front was dire. In the Munich box office they were not talking about thousands, hundreds or even scores of sales. Orders were dribbling in in ones or twos. My job, I knew, was to build up Richard's profile so that even the many sceptics out there would start to believe he had what Our Enery called 'a puncher's chance'.

'Tell me about your childhood,' I said, hoping to get some material to dress up his modern Cinderella Man image. He did not disappoint, and here verbatim – hear it in heavy Yorkshire dialect – is the picture that he painted about his life before boxing, 'My childhood made Oliver Twist seem privileged. Didn't know my father – my real father – despite what my mother may say. Have a look at my ten siblings, all younger than me. They're all short and dark, and none have my height and sandy-ginger colouring.

'I were pushed from pillar to post when I were a kid, and spent a lot of time in children's homes. Drank from a bottle of bleach when I were a toddler and it gave me a speech impediment. If you'd been doing this interview when I were a school kid, I'd have covered your notebook in spit because I had an uncontrollable stutter.

'You can imagine the piss-taking that I had to face, and t'only way I could shut it up were to lash out. I had good answers in my head but couldn't get them out because of my stutter. So bloody frustrating. I wanted to murder people who mimicked me. N-n-n-nothing I could do about it [he was not acting]. I thought, "I'll show 'em." Well now I have. I'm going to fight for t'biggest prize in sport and against t'most famous boxer in history. Yea, I'll show 'em. D-D-Dickie Dunn has done good.

'The stammer still comes out now and again when I'm excited but I conquered it thanks to our lass, Janet. She's t'best thing ever happened to me. I used to get into all sorts of scrapes before I met her. I were angry and wanted to fight t'world. I weren't a villain, just a yob who were always getting up to mischief. It were Janet who taught me to be more responsible and respectful.

'My dream were to be a rugby league star and didn't really take boxing seriously until I were into my 20s. Found I were quite useful and Jimmy here is a great teacher. It were Janet who made up my mind between boxing and rugby league. She burnt my rugby boots! New they were. Cost me a fiver, but she said I had to choose and reckoned I were a better boxer than I were a rugby player. Tossed the boots on the fire, without a by-your-word. That were it then, I were going to be a boxer.

'Jan's got two brothers who are professionals, and I give them piggy backs when I'm on training runs. Strengthens the calf muscles. They're my greatest fans, and I cheer them on when they're in the ring.

'I'm not a natural southpaw, but just adopted the style to be awkward. That's me. An awkward cuss. When I were in New York last week I overheard Ali's trainer Angelo Dundee saying he thought southpaws should be drowned at birth. Lefties he called them. That's great to know he thinks like that. Shows Ali does not fancy fighting southpaws.

'I remember that Germany's Karl Mildenberger gave him all sorts of problems. He's a leftie like me but does not have my punching power. There were a time, three or so years back, when I were going to give up boxing. I'd become disillusioned after three defeats when I were fighting with one hand 'cos I'd broken a bone. Jan gave me a good talking to. Called me a coward and said I were running away. She were right, and I decided to give it one more go. Now look at me.

'I still consider Jimmy my guv'nor, even though I now fight under the George Biddles banner. Pop and me are very close and I know he'll always look after my interests. He could only take me so far as a professional, because he didn't have t'contacts. That's why we went to George Biddles to manage us. He's been around for centuries and knows all t'people who matter in't big business world of boxing.

'The biggest plus for us when we joined t'Biddles stable is that I were able to get good-quality sparring. We could never get heavyweight boxers to come up here to Bradford to help me sharpen up. You'll see from my record that it started to improve t'minute I began getting regular sparring sessions with blokes my size. It takes a good big 'un to get t'best out of a good big 'un. One of Pop's sayings.

'The gym we built up here is like a second home to me. I work hard and spar for speed with Jimmy's sons, without taking liberties with them. Both are much smaller than me but they get me moving quickly and nimbly. And I run and run for miles, Jimmy following on his small putt-putt motorbike. Boxing is as much about legs as fists. The stronger your legs and your stamina t'easier it becomes. Ali has proved that throughout his career, but he was clearly not in shape against Jimmy Young. I just hope he is as slow and heavy against me.

'I've been an Ali fan since his Cassius Clay days, and a gypsy once read my palm when I were visiting Blackpool on a day out and she said I were going to fight Clay, as he were then. She told me I were going to become heavyweight champion of the world. Think she were after a big tip.

'Best thing I discovered were t'Territorial Army and I look on the parachute regiment as family. I've never been afraid of hard work and have grafted on farms, building sites and am now a fully qualified scaffolder. The money I'm earning from the Ali fight will set me, Janet and the kids, up for life. We have big business plans that I shall keep to myself until I retire from t'ring.

'I pride myself on my strength, staying power and I can bang with t'best of them. Ask that Bernd August feller. He was a tall, handsome chap at the start of our fight, and within three rounds I had him looking as if he'd been in a car smash.

'I'm not stupid enough to think I'm better than Ali. Who is? He has been The Master for many years. But every dog has its day and, believe me, I am a very hungry dog. I'm going to give Muhammad Ali t'fright of his life. Think I could be getting into t'ring with him at just t'reet time.'

I left out the sensitive stuff about Richard claiming not to have known his real father when I released my interview to the provincial papers, but – as you will learn – it was a statement that was to come back to haunt us later in our association.

On my return to my London base, there was a message to call Jarvis Astaire. He sounded agitated.

'Theatre ticket sales are picking up,' he reported, with gloom rather than glee in his voice. 'That's the good news. The bad news is there may not be a fight. The German syndicate have got cold feet, but it's too late to switch the show to the UK. Ali is on a world tour promoting his autobiography and has two key dates lined up after the Dunn fight – a box-wrestling match with Japanese wrestler Antonio Inoki in June and then a showdown fight with Ken Norton in September.'

'Uh, what if Richard beats Ali?' I asked, throwing a pebble in the pool.

There was a pause on the line followed by a chuckle and then prolonged laughter.

'Norman, if that happens,' Jarvis said in that precise way of his, 'I'll run naked around Wembley Stadium.'

'Can I be the publicist?' I asked. 'For that I could sell tickets.'

Last word to Jarvis, 'I'll get my secretary to bike you the necessary air tickets. You're booked on the flight to Munich on 11 May with Dunn's entourage. There are eight of you altogether, including three sparring partners and George Biddles and Jimmy Devanney. Oh yes, and Mickey Duff. The two of you will be sharing a room at the Munich Hilton. Enjoy.'

Round Four

Lead on Mick Duff

MICKEY DUFF! One of the most charismatic, interesting, irritating, dynamic, volcanic, self-obsessed, intelligent, scheming, belligerent, charming-when-it-mattered, bullying, relentless, energetic, neurotic, successful characters ever to cross my path. I shall spend quite a time introducing you to Mickey before we get to our adventures in Munich, because he was such a tour de force in my world.

I first came across the young Mickey in his hustling days, when he and his brother-in-law Henry Simmons used to sell perfumed water to gullible shoppers from the back of a van in the East End's bustling Petticoat Lane market in the 1950s. They would pass around a genuine bottle of Chanel perfume for punters to sniff and then con them into buying doctored bottles filled with scented tap water at half a crown a time (2s 6d, or 12.5p). It was right out of *Only Fools and Horses*. Scriptwriter John Sullivan would have had a feast with Mickey Duff anecdotes.

Born Monek Prager in Poland in 1929 into an Hasidic Jewish family, he was the son of a Rabbi and escaped to Britain in 1938 just months ahead of the German invasion that led to many of his family perishing in the extermination camps. He briefly studied to become a Rabbi at a Jewish school in Gateshead but found boxing a better attraction and came south to an East End ghetto, where he thrived on the everyday challenge of life. 'We lived like rats and I was determined to be King Rat,' he told me when I worked with him on an autobiography that didn't make it to publication because he considered the £5,000 advance money an insult.

He claimed he borrowed the Mickey Duff moniker from a hoodlum in a James Cagney gangster film, although no amount of research can come up with such a character in any cast list. He said he adopted the name so that he could box professionally from the age of 15 without his parents knowing.

'I was keen on taking the money but not the punches,' said Mickey, with a flattened nose as evidence that he did not always meet his target during his 69-fight, five-year career as a 9st and then 10st boxer in which he never made it beyond contender status. 'I wouldn't have booked me. I used to stink the place out by running backwards around the ring. Hit but don't get hit was my motto.'

He used to box with a Star of David on his shorts, 'Not because I was promoting my religion but because I attracted Jewish gamblers and I used to do business with them.' Occasionally he threw a fight to get extra money from the bookmakers, but he swore that since going legitimate as a matchmaker/promoter he had never been involved in a 'bent' fight.

By the time we became friends in the 1950s, he was selling Singer sewing machines to the East End sweatshops and scrabbling a living manufacturing duffel coats, while in his spare time building a reputation as a boxing matchmaker who knew a good fight before he saw it. Of course, he went on to become one of the most powerful forces in world boxing and was established as 'the man to go to' on both sides of the Atlantic. I hung on to his coat-tails and worked as a PR for him and his partners Harry Levene, Jarvis Astaire and Mike Barrett, and with my best pal, the boxing manager supreme, Terry Lawless, in our corner.

While Astaire used words as carefully as if they were rationed, Mickey was accompanied by armies of them and used to send them into battle at the first hint of disagreement. In my long career as a listener and observer – OK, snoop – I've never known anybody have so many arguments and disputes as Mickey. He thrived on winning shouting matches, yet also had a side of him when he could quietly charm the birds down out of the trees and then get them singing to his tune.

It was a well-kept secret that Mickey was stateless under British citizenship law until he co-promoted the Muhammad Ali–Henry Cooper heavyweight world title fight at Highbury in May 1966. Mickey became British on his 37th birthday after his nemesis Jack Solomons had ruthlessly tried to block him obtaining a promoter's licence on the grounds that he was 'a foreigner'.

The Ali–Cooper fight, a huge box office and television winner, marked the end of the Solomons ascendancy over British boxing. For Mickey there was suddenly the sweet smell of success, and not from a whiff of perfumed tap water. He told me, 'Solomons accused us of running a syndicate, not seeing the irony that he'd virtually had a one-man monopoly for 20 years after the war. At least we shared our cake.'

I helped with the publicity when Mickey launched the Anglo-American Sporting Club, in the 1960s, based at the London Hilton. The notorious Kray twins applied for membership, a couple of weeks after interviewing me for the role of their part-time publicist. Mickey had the balls – some would say the lunacy – to turn down their application on the grounds that 'they were not appropriate clientele'.

His then wife, Marie, rang me at the club office one morning in a distressed state to say, 'Mickey's on his way in. Tell him I've just been sent four dead rats in a flower box.' Mickey had already heard, and said, 'That can only be the Krays. I'll send them a telegram that says, "No rats allowed."'

Instead, he reported the twins to his mate at Scotland Yard, Leonard 'Nipper' Read, who had been investigating the affairs of the Krays for three years. The following week they were arrested and eventually locked up following a harrowing trial at the Old Bailey. Read, with Mickey's backing, later became chairman of the British Boxing Board of Control. The Krays were banged up for 30 years each. Now that would have tested my PR skills. A year on, Mickey was being given a late-night lift after a show in Germany by a Berlin promoter, who said in conversational tone, 'Mickey, please let me assure you that all the talk of the Holocaust is exaggerated to make we Germans seem inhuman. We did not kill six million Jews. No more than two million, tops.'

Duff said, 'Stop the car. Now!' He got out in the middle of nowhere and found his own way back to his hotel.

Mickey had the head of an accountant and the heart of an executioner. 'If you want loyalty,' he would say, 'buy a dog.' He once fell out with a boxer he steered to a world title but kept managing him, telling associates, 'He's a bastard – but he's *my* bastard.'

Because he had studied the Bible and Hebrew Scriptures in depth, Mickey was quite the philosopher and once told me after I had written a scathing piece about one of his promotions, 'It's easy to be wise in words. Better to be wise in deeds.'

His gambling, in casinos and at the card table, was legendary and it was nothing for him to win or lose £20,000 in one sitting, often into the early hours of the morning. He had VIP status at Las Vegas hotels that only went to the highest of high rollers. Nobody ever knew whether he had won or lost. 'I've got a poker face and a poker player's mentality,' he told me. 'Win or lose, I get the same emotion. I convince myself it's only money and just sit and wait for the next roll of the dice. That's life.'

I realised that he had not changed since those early days when his patter at Petticoat Lane was, 'I'm not asking you for a pound for this exclusive perfume, madam, not even ten bob; it's yours provided you buy it right now for just half a crown. Come on, it's only money.'

He could be wise, wild, wicked, witty and withering all in the spate of one thought process, was never dull, and was happiest when he had news or a joke to share. He would always start off by saying, 'Have I got news for you,' or, 'Have I got a joke for you.' I always found him entertaining but often almost overwhelming, rolling over you with his powerful personality and, fittingly, his punchlines.

Yes, as I often used to say to him which appealed to his gigantic ego, 'Lead on Mick Duff'.

* * *

So this was the mesmerising Mickey Duff with whom I was going to spend two weeks sharing a room in the Munich Hilton, which was also the headquarters for the promoters of the Ali–Dunn fight.

What a pantomime we had getting out there.

We checked in at Heathrow along with Richard Dunn, his father-in-law and trainer Jimmy Devanney and his septuagenarian manager George Biddles. Also boarding were sparring partners Neville Meade, Eddie Fenton and Derek Simpkin, while German-based Nigerian champion Ngozika Ekwelum was due to join the Dunn camp in Munich.

The first call came for our flight and Mickey was conspicuous by his absence. He had gone to duty free for cigarettes. As Richard and company made their way to the departure lounge there was another call, and I decided to locate Mickey.

I dragged him from duty free, and just as we were about to rejoin the Dunn party, Mickey suddenly realised he had left his wallet at the cash counter. By the time we chased back, the wallet had been handed in to airport security. Now Mickey had to prove who he was and, of course, all his identity material was in the wallet that was lumped together with his passport, gold American Express credit card and boarding pass.

Mickey being Mickey, he became over-aggressive and got involved in a slanging match with the jobsworth security officers, who did not take kindly to his 'Do you know who I am?' attitude. By the time he convinced them he was the man in the passport photograph – yes, it was one of *those* photos that look nothing like the holder – they were announcing the last call for our flight.

'We'll be all right,' said Mickey, who had regained his composure and was talking with the experience of making more international flights than most pilots. 'We've checked in. They won't go without us.'

Wrong!

They had just closed the gates as we got to the departure lounge, and no amount of pleading and shouting could convince the uniformed staff to open them and let us on board the plane carrying world title challenger Richard Dunn, who we were supposed to introduce to the press at Munich airport. Mickey actually managed to induce tears as he cried in a last desperate bid to get the pilot to be asked to allow us on, but we were left watching the plane taxi and take off with our luggage but not us. I could only imagine the thoughts going through the mind of the veteran George Biddles as he looked around the aircraft to find no sign of Mickey or me.

Quite a start to our Munich adventure.

* * *

A slowly calmed-down Mickey and I eventually arrived in Munich two hours later on a following flight, by which time the depleted Dunn entourage was checking into the Hilton Hotel. A harassed George Biddles told us that there was little interest in Richard's arrival and that the poorly attended press conference had lasted just ten minutes. I scrunched up the hand-written notes I had for Richard in which I had him telling the reporters, 'I have come not to praise Ali but to bury him. There will be no peace in our time for him here in Munich.'

Over the top? I was wearing my publicist's hat, remember. No holds barred when you had to get bums on seats.

Mickey and I had barely checked into our hotel room when the telephone rang. I answered. It was an angry-sounding George Biddles.' 'Put Mickey on,' he snapped.

I handed the receiver to Mickey, and was now only hearing his responses. 'What d'you mean, you're going home?'

Mickey was now back into shouting mode, just as he had been with the security men at the airport. 'But we'll get sued for every dollar we've got.' He was now talking at rather than to Biddles. 'You can't fly back now. We're contracted to promote the fight here for two weeks.'

Mickey was now shouting so loudly that I felt he didn't need the phone because Biddles was staying in the same building. 'I'll meet you in the foyer in two minutes. I'm gonna kick ass.'

I should point out that Mickey spent much of his time in the States and often used their colourful language.

Mickey threw down the receiver and I followed him to the foyer from our tenth-floor room into which we had only just walked. Biddles, looking every one of his 72 years, was already there alongside Jimmy Devanney, who was all but hopping with suppressed anger.

'They're taking us for reet mugs,' Devanney said before Mickey could get a word out. 'They've given us a gym – well, a room – for our training and it's got nowt in it but a couple of skipping ropes and a medicine ball. Not even a punchbag.'

'We've told them we'll go home and finish our training in a proper gym in England and we'll come back the day before the fight,' Biddles said in a strong East Midlands accent that had never changed in a 50-year career as a Leicester-based boxing promoter and manager.

A squat, overweight, perspiring representative of the Munich-based promotion syndicate arrived, and Mickey piled straight into him in fluent German with a rich mixture of Yiddish. I managed to pick out a few of the more colourful words, such as schmuck, meshuggeneh, miststuck and arschloch. For those of you unable to match my schoolboy Deutsch, Mickey was putting his tongue to such descriptive words as stupid, foolish, bastard and arsehole.

He left the German promoter in no doubt that the championship challenger would return home if better training facilities were not offered immediately.

Within an hour, the promoters had come up with a nearby gymnasium that had all the necessary equipment. Crisis over. Now Mickey and I could unpack our luggage.

It was good to be in Munich!

* * *

That evening we had our first 'ideas' meeting in the grim knowledge that the promotion was, to quote Mickey, 'dying on its arse'. We met in a private room laid on by the hotel, with Mickey in the chair, a wheezing George Biddles, bookworm Jimmy Devanney, Ersnt Schoener, the spokesman for the Munich promoters, me with my notebook, and Richard Dunn, who was almost falling asleep after completing his daily eight-mile run around the nearby Englischer Garten.

'Very pretty but not half as bracing or challenging as t'moors,' he reported. 'We have hills there that are like mountains. Great for t'stamina.' Schoener (not his real name, I am protecting him from being a laughing stock) reported that the promotion stood to lose 'millions of dollars' unless there was a sudden rush of interest. 'Not only are ve not selling tickets but the European television companies are not prepared to cover zer fight because zey do not zink Dunn has a chance.'

It was a brutal thing to say in front of Richard (I could never bring myself to call him Dick), but he was past caring and was dozing in his chair. 'Ve need to generate interest among zose citizens of Munich who haf no interest in boxing but are perhaps Anglophiles,' said Schoener, with a German accent that could have come out of Ealing comedy casting. 'Do you haf any contact with your Crown Prince Charles? Ve vould happily velcome him here as our ringside guest of honour.'

'You've got as much chance of that,' said Mickey, with a mix of irritation and amusement, 'as the Chief Rabbi going to tea with Yasser Arafat. Zilch.'

'How about zer Beatles?' asked an uncrushable Schoener. 'It vas here in Germany zey ver discovered. In Hamburg. Ve vould velcome them mit open arms.'

'They broke up years ago, you schmuck,' Mickey spat out, his patience at breaking point. 'Prince Charles, the Beatles. Which world are you living in? We need to attract punters, not non-paying VIPs.'

He then threw me in at the deep end. 'So Norm, what ideas have you got in that computer brain of yours?' he asked. 'Have you got a rabbit you can produce from your hat?'

'Bugs Bunny couldn't come up with a story to save this show,' I replied. 'The only way we could attract spectators is to convince them that Richard has a chance.'

'Wouldn't have come out here if I didn't think I could win it,' Richard said with a positivity that visibly shocked Schoener.

'Rather you zan me,' he responded. 'Couldn't pay me to get in zer ring with Ali. I saw vat he did to our Karl Mildenberger. And he could *really* fight.'

That lit Igor's fuse. 'Hey, we don't want your bloody negativity in here,' Jimmy Devanney said with a sudden eruption. 'Richard is in great condition, both physically and psychologically. We can do without idiots like you undermining his confidence. We've got a plan and Ali will not find this a pushover. We're not Joe Bugner, here to dance. We're here to fight.'

'I'm gonna give it my all,' Richard added as Schoener departed, leaving the mad Englishmen alone with their dreams.

Somebody, it may have been me, suggested that Richard considered doing something that nobody had achieved against Ali – getting himself disqualified. 'If your plan of beating him with aggressive tactics is not working,' I said, wondering if I was losing it, 'you could try tipping him out of the ring when he performs his rope-a-dope. Firpo, the Wild Bull of the Pampas, did it against Jack Dempsey in 1923. It could earn you a return fight.'

'Yes,' said Mickey, who had an encyclopaedic knowledge of boxing history, 'and then Dempsey got back in the ring and knocked ten skittles out of the Argentinian.'

'Sounds barmy to me,' said George Biddles, who had seen it all and done it all in his 50 years in the fight game. 'George Foreman couldn't shift him off the ropes and he hit him with everything but the ring stool. No, we've got to go for a shock start, like Richard did against August.'

'Our plan is to swarm all over Ali before he has time to settle into that dancing rhythm of his,' said Devanney, promoting himself from Igor to Dr Frankenstein. 'Richard is strong enough and fit enough to do it. This is not the Ali of old. He showed against Jimmy Young in his last fight that he's nowt like the champion he were.'

I handed Richard an A4 sheet of paper on which I had typed a quote that I wanted him to learn for the press conference we had planned for when the British press gang arrived. 'I'd like to release this tomorrow,' I said, as he read it aloud:

'Ever since I knew I were challenging Muhammad Ali for his world title, I've had a recurring dream. We're fighting here in Munich, and he's leaning back on't ropes like he did against George Foreman. It's the eighth round and t'crowd is going crazy as Ali bounces off t'ropes towards me. I catch him with a left-right combination to t'jaw and he falls backwards and out of the ring. By the time he scrambles back he's counted out and our lass, Janet, is holding my right arm aloft and I wake up with a big smile on my face feeling reet champion.'

I braced myself ready for an argument as to whether we wanted to go down the hackneyed dream road when Richard added, 'Bloody 'ell, Norm, you been listening in on my dreams? This is almost exactly what I've been dreaming, except I have no idea what round it is and our lass doesn't appear but it's Jimmy who's holding my arm up in victory.'

George Biddles sniffed. He'd seen it all before. 'We pulled the same publicity stunt,' he recalled, 'when I managed Hogan Kid Bassey in his world featherweight title fight against Cherif Hamia in 1957. We told the press Hogan had dreamed of winning in the tenth round – and that's exactly what he did. Our story put doubts in Hamia's mind and he came apart in that tenth round.'

'Don't think it'll cost Ali sleep,' Mickey said cynically, 'but it's worth a shot just to get it into the minds of punters that there are two men in the ring. When Ali fights he tends to take all the attention. Watch the way the publicity and buzz shoots up when he arrives later this week. With the greatest respect, Richard, it's Ali everybody wants to see.'

Not quite everybody. There were several million West Germans who were not interested.

Having got my 'dream fight' idea accepted, I sensed this was not the right time to reveal that I did have a rabbit in my hat.

His name was Romark, and I would spring him on Richard when the time was right. What's up, doc?

Round Five

The odd couple

IT QUICKLY became apparent that Mickey and I together in one room was like the remaking of Neil Simon's 1960s hit comedy *The Odd Couple*. I was the neat, pedantic Felix and Mickey definitely the untidy, slovenly Oscar. 'If everybody was as spic and span as you, hotel maids would be put out of work,' was his take on my tidiness. He just dropped clothes where he stood, and his twin bed after our first night looked as if he'd been in a wrestling match. But he was fussy, fastidious even, about his appearance, and would spend up to 20 minutes in front of the mirror quiffing and combing over what was left of his near-orange dyed hair.

Mickey lived on the telephone. This was before the 1980s arrival of the mobile, and he was continually making and taking calls in his room, at reception, right across the hotel and at the gymnasium. 'Telefunken für Herr Duff' became a catchphrase in the Richard Dunn camp.

His most regular conversations were with Jarvis Astaire in London and Top Rank CEO Bob Arum in the States. Top Rank had put the fight together for screening on NBC, and all financial transactions with the German promoters were going through Arum, a Harvard-educated lawyer. He shared the orthodox Jewish background of both Mickey and Jarvis, and their telephone talks were punctuated with Yiddish philosophy and business acumen.

I was only hearing Mickey's end of things. He didn't shout or scream at Arum, and after one of their early exchanges he put the telephone down with a resigned air.

'Have I got news for you,' he said, with rare defeatism in his voice. 'Just been told our hotel bills haven't been pre-paid as agreed and we're being kicked out if the German promoters don't put up the promised money by midday. I'm certainly not going to pay. This is their gig.'

I had just telexed the Richard Dunn 'eighth round dream victory' story to the main British news agencies Press Association and Exchange Telegraph, and was now dealing with a nightmare.

The previous evening over dinner with the Dunn party in the main Hilton restaurant, we had been introduced to Nigerian heavyweight champion Ngozika Ekwelum. He had arrived from his Berlin base as an extra sparring partner for a down payment fee of £200, plus £20 a round.

This brought instant tension to the dining table, because just two years earlier in a Berlin ring Ekwelum had bombed Richard to defeat in seven rounds, and the ultra-confident, boastful 28-year-old made no secret of the fact that he felt he should have been the one challenging Ali.

Richard and Jimmy Devanney quietly had their own private joke, referring to Ekwelum behind his back as Ecky Thump, a catchphrase from the popular *Goodies* television show.

The fighter from Lagos sensed that they were laughing at his expense. 'You are a very fortunate man, Mr Dunn,' he announced, loud enough for all diners on nearby tables to hear. 'It is I who should be fighting Muhammad Ali.'

'You couldn't fill a telephone box with spectators,' Mickey said with characteristic bluntness, conveniently forgetting that they were hardly battering down the doors to see Richard.

'Mr Dunn has got the right complexion and connection,' a bitter Ekwelum said in a precise English accent that carried heavy West African and German overtones. 'I will challenge the winner to meet me and give me the shot at the title I deserve. It is time Africa had the championship.'

Veteran manager George Biddles nodded wisely. 'I've booked you for sparring, lad, to get Richard mad,' he said. 'I want to get him angry, ready for Ali. He's become too nice since he clinched the fight. I want him mean and nasty on the big night. So get him mad.'

We didn't know just how literally Ekwelum was going to take this instruction.

There was a welcome break to the sudden intensity when Mickey ordered a bottle of water. The German waiter asked innocently, 'Mit gas?'

Mickey, who had lost relatives at the nearby Dachau concentration camp, replied, 'You must be fucking joking.'

* * *

Our hotel room deposits were paid promptly at midday and Mickey and I – immediate crisis over – strolled to the nearby gymnasium to watch Richard sparring. First of all three rounds each with Neville Meade, Derek Simpkin and then Eddie Fenton, each of them impersonating Ali with swift dancing and jabbing on the retreat. Next it was the turn of the mightily muscled Ekwelum.

There was a sparse audience of 50 or so German spectators, casually passing an hour while watching to see what the little-known British challenger had to offer. When they saw their adopted hero climb into the ring they started to chant his name as if he were the main man.

Ekwelum, wearing huge 18oz sparring gloves, responded by forgetting he was there to impersonate Ali and fought like a contender for the title. His right hand punch was feared throughout the heavyweight boxing division, and Richard – head guard skew-whiff – found himself having to desperately defend himself.

Suddenly, Ekwelum crossed a sizzling right to the jaw which made an Ecky Thumping sound as it landed. Richard's knees buckled and he went on a walkabout with scattered senses. He was out on his feet.

George Biddles, standing outside the ring, instantly rang the bell to end the round even though these was another full minute to go.

Mickey Duff, alongside me and suddenly looking as if he too had taken a punch to the chin, said, 'Norman, no way can you report this. The half a dozen people who have bought tickets will want their money back. Dunn's jaw is made of glass.'

Ekwelum did not appear at our hotel again and the next we heard he was back in Berlin. No doubt mit laughing gas.

* * *

After dinner that evening I decided it was time to sell my Romark idea to Richard, Jimmy Devanney and George Biddles. Mickey had gone off to the local casino, where he spent more time than at the fight headquarters, often staying until the early hours. We became like chips (my little joke) that passed in the night.

'I've got an idea that might convince you of my insanity,' I said to Richard, with his manager and trainer ready to jump on me if I mentioned anything that could further dent confidence that had been damaged by the thump from Ekwelum.

I took a deep breath and went for it. 'I want to bring over a man from London to try hypnotising you,' I said, rushing my words. 'His name is Romark and he has a history of helping sportsmen.'

Jimmy Devanney was first to react. 'Romark?' he repeated parrot fashion. 'Isn't he the nutcase who tried to drive across London blindfolded?' I shuffled in embarrassment. 'Yes, that's the one,' I conceded with a sudden loss of confidence in my idea. 'But he's got an impressive record with stunts that were successful.'

Time for George Biddles to have his say. 'Hardly original,' he said, continuing the 'been-there-done-that' stance of somebody who had seen and done it all. 'I remember Eric "Boy" Boon being hypnotised into thinking he could win in his return fight with Arthur Danahar back in the 1940s. Danahar knocked him cold in the tenth round.'

'I think you're fucking crackers,' was the fairly emphatic response from Richard Dunn, the only one whose opinion really mattered.

I was about to retreat defeated to my corner when Biddles came to my rescue.

'I know your role is to publicise the fight,' he said, 'and just the suggestion that Richard is being hypnotised could bring in a few more customers. And it just might make Ali think twice. Anything that plants the slightest doubt in his mind must be a plus for us.'

Richard nodded that big, wide, sandy-blond head of his. 'True,' he said. 'It'll get people thinking. Let's go for it.'

I told Mickey the plan when he returned from the casino at two o'clock in the morning with a thick wad of Deutsche Marks to show it had been a good session at the tables.

'It would take Sigmund Freud to convince Richard he has a chance against Ali,' he said, stuffing his winnings under a false bottom in his suitcase. 'But if it gets the fight mentioned in the papers it's worth it. So far it's the quietest build-up I've ever known for a world heavyweight title fight. Nobody gives Richard a gnat's chance in hell.'

All I had to do now was to find a way of getting Romark to Munich. We couldn't risk letting him drive out blindfolded.

My first call the next morning was to my old press box colleague Ron Wills at the *Daily Mirror*. He had led the way on the Romark–Crystal Palace saga and he gave me the illusionist's home telephone number. 'He's as mad as a hatter,' Ron warned, 'but he'd sell his grandmother for publicity. If you're going to do anything with him for the Ali–Dunn fight, let me know so that I can get the *Mirror* involved.'

This was beginning to sound like an idea that could get off the ground, and if I could get the *Mirror* to pay all his travel and hotel expenses I knew that would put me in the good books of Jarvis and Mickey.

* * *

Here, verbatim, is my telephone conversation with Ronald Markham, alias Romark:

'Ronald Markham?'

'He's not here. Who's this?'

'It's Norman Giller, publicist for the upcoming Muhammad Ali–Richard Dunn fight.'

'Just a second; I'll put Romark on.' Moments later, in exactly the same voice, 'Romark here. What can I do for you?'

'I'm Norman Giller here in Munich, working as publicist for the Muhammad Ali–Richard Dunn world heavyweight championship fight.'

'You want my prediction? I'm afraid that will cost you.'

'Not exactly. I was just wondering if you'd be interested in perhaps hypnotising Richard before the fight?'

There then followed a dramatic pause of several seconds when even I wondered if those words had just dropped from my lips.

'Is this a leg pull?'

'No. I'm genuinely asking on behalf of Richard and his manager George Biddles.'

'Sorry to sound suspicious. Just last week I had somebody purporting to be from the BBC ringing me up and asking if I'd be willing to hypnotise Prince Charles. Turned out to be a prank.'

'I can understand your caution. So many cranks around.'

'Exactly. I have been accused of being a crank myself, but that's because I take on crazy challenges. Convincing Richard Dunn that he can defeat Muhammad Ali would come into that category.'

'Have you ever hypnotised a boxer?'

'No, football has been more my sport. I could give you a catalogue of managers and players I've helped.'

'I don't think Malcolm Allison would give you a recommendation.'

'Below the belt, old chap. Mr Allison and I are going through legal channels against each other. I invited him to my Harley Street offices to settle matters once and for all, but he did not turn up for our appointment. I put a curse on his Crystal Palace team and that is why they lost just last month to Southampton in the semi-final of the FA Cup. The moral of the story is, "Don't upset Romark."'

'The bottom line, Mr Markham …'

'Romark, please.'

'... is are you free to come out here to Munich to have some sessions with Richard Dunn before his title challenge against Muhammad Ali?'

'There would need to be a fee and expenses, of course.'

'Of course. I will arrange with the *Daily Mirror* to organise this in return for an exclusive photo opportunity and story once you get out here.'

'I have cooperated with them before on the original Crystal Palace project. I worked for several weeks with the Palace players and had them believing in themselves but Mr Allison went back on his word and refused to pay me my agreed fee. Romark was not happy.'

'Somebody from the *Mirror*, probably Ron Wills, will be in touch with you shortly to make arrangements for you to join us out here. I look forward to meeting you face to face.'

'The pleasure will be mine, Mr Giller.'

I could almost taste the oil coming down the line as I replaced the telephone receiver.

Next, back to Ron Wills with the news that Romark was ready to cooperate with the *Mirror* in return for a fee and travel and hotel expenses.

They settled on a fee of £1,000 plus expenses. In return I had to agree to them having first announcement of Romark putting Dunn under hypnosis, plus an exclusive photograph of Richard and Romark together.

I could arrange that, provided Richard played ball.

We had a new odd couple – Richard Dunn and Romark.

Round Six

The Ali circus hits town

THE ARRIVAL of Muhammad Ali brought sudden excitement and great expectations to where there had been only despondency and despair. You could actually *feel* the atmosphere lift when he swaggered into Munich accompanied by an entourage of 54 helpers, healers, hawkers, hucksters and hangers-on. I had travelled the world covering major sporting events but had never witnessed anything quite like the Ali circus coming to town. They took over Munich like an invading army.

Ali's management had chartered a flight from the United States, and virtually every one of the passengers was on the fighter's payroll and/or expense sheet. They filled 40 rooms in the five-star Bayerischer Hof hotel and another ten in the Munich Hilton, where the relatively small Dunn party was camped.

Throughout his stay, I noted that Ali never changed his wristwatch from US time. He ate breakfast in the evening and dinner in the morning, and while everybody thought he was not training he would go to the gymnasium in the middle of the night. I witnessed him knocking lumps off his white sparring partner Rodney Bobick, while taking it easy on his four black hired accomplices, including former heavyweight champion Jimmy Ellis, who had been forced to retire with a damaged retina. Ali carefully hit him only in the body.

It was noticeable that he did not have a southpaw among his sparring partners. When I put that to him, Ali just shrugged and said, 'Southpaw, north paw, east paw, west paw, I'm gonna knock your boy clean out. Have you told him he's fighting the greatest heavyweight the world has ever seen?'

Ali saw me as a vessel to get to Richard. I had worked with him on three previous fights and there was mutual respect but he knew I was in Dunn's corner. I say respect. In truth I idolised the man. For me, he was and remains the greatest sporting personality of them all.

People are always asking me what the *real* Muhammad Ali was like. Having been privileged to spend hours in his company, I can tell you that there were at least three of him. There was the brash, flash Louisville Lip who would say anything to sell tickets, the caring humanitarian and sincerely religious Muslim, and the one I liked best of all, inquisitive, quietly spoken and more interested in listening to you than talking about himself. But put a microphone near him and he went into sales pitch, and he made no secret that as important as it was promoting his title fight with Dunn, publicising his recently published autobiography, *The Greatest*, was just as crucial.

'I've just completed a world tour selling my book,' he told me during a training break, 'and, man, I'm exhausted. I'd much rather be fightin' than writin'. You're a words man and know that getting it all down on paper is much harder than just talkin'.' He did not mention the part his ghostwriters Richard Durham and Toni Morrison played.

We chatted for an hour while I got material for the fact files that I was preparing for the pending arrival of the British press contingent. 'My reputation's on the line here,' he said. 'I'm told very few tickets have been sold. That looks bad for me. Not my fault nobody's heard of your Richard Dunn. I'm gonna make him famous by knocking him all the way back to Yorkshire.'

What concerned me during my talk with Ali – I called him 'Champ' – was the slight slur to his speech that had not been there the last time we had chatted before his 1975 'Thrilla in Manila' with Joe Frazier. I asked after his health and he responded in trademark rhyme, 'Muhammad Ali is as fit as can be; he's ready to dance 15 rounds; just you make sure you're in your seat to see; it'll be even better than it sounds.'

The huge smile that followed was the old, loveable Ali, and – silly me – I welled up.

The next morning, over coffee with Mickey and Ali's hugely respected personal physician and close confidant, Dr Ferdie Pacheco, I put it to the man known as 'The Fight Doctor' that Ali was showing signs of his ring wars. Pacheco, a renowned artist with the paintbrush when he was not working in Ali's corner, leant forward confidentially and talked to Mickey and me in the hushed tones of somebody carrying a weight on his back, 'I've been telling the Champ for months that it's time to quit. He and Frazier nearly killed each other in Manila. That was the time to get out. No human body can take the sort of punishment Ali absorbs. All those body shots from George Foreman, the wars with Norton and Frazier. It's all beginning to take its toll. I've told him if he doesn't quit then he can carry on without me. He was a shadow of the real Ali against Jimmy Young. Your guy just might be getting him at the right time.'

Dr Pacheco looked around the hotel restaurant at the dozens of people eating and drinking at Ali's expense. 'Look at all these leeches,' he said, with quiet loathing, 'they're all feeding off the Champ. Not one of them will be honest and tell him the party's over. He's their meal ticket. Without him, they are nobodies. There are more than 40 here just taking a free ride and giving nothing in return. Ali is the easiest touch there will ever be. He would give away his last cent. And this lot would take it.'

Bobby Goodman, Ali's travelling PR and son of the legendary fight publicist Murray Goodman, was open-mouthed with amazement at the lack of interest generated by the German promoters. 'They have not even bothered to get flyers printed,' he grumbled. 'It's being run by a bunch of goddam amateurs. I'm going to do my best to drum up publicity, but I've got a feeling this show is dead in the water.'

He went off for a game of golf with his old Limey chum Reg Gutteridge, a fascinating, larger-than-life character who encouraged me to get out into the big wide world as a journalist when I was his copy boy on London's *Evening News* back in the 1950s. Reg, son of Dick Gutteridge, one of boxing's famous Gutteridge twins, was an exceptional amateur prospect when he lost a leg in the Normandy Landings of 1944. He had the character to change direction from a boxing career to become an exceptional sportswriter and the best-informed ringside commentator in the business.

I caught up with Bobby later and asked how the golf had gone. 'That Reg Gutteridge!' he exclaimed. 'I hit what I thought was a perfect shot off the tee on the short fifth but didn't see where the ball went. Reggie puts his ball down on the tee and says very casually, "So I need this for a half." I'd got my first ever hole in one and that Limey so-and-so didn't let me celebrate.'

They remained the best of buddies and each became a member of the renowned American Boxing Hall of Fame. That sure beats a hole in one.

* * *

Ali's third morning in Munich dawned with Mickey getting a call from Arum saying that Top Rank were preparing to pull the plug on the fight. 'The Germans have failed to come up with a contracted $250,000 to cover his taxes,' he said. 'I've told Ali and he says he's quite happy to come home.'

Mickey immediately telephoned Jarvis, and within an hour he had persuaded the German company to come up with the outstanding money under the threat that he would sue them for ten times the amount if the fight fell through.

Ali immediately ordered $200,000 of tickets, which he paid for, then he went to the local American military camps and handed out fistfuls of free passes to the troops. Back home it was a philanthropic act that brought savage criticism from the many Ali haters. They pointed out the irony of a man who had refused to fight for his country against the Vietcong giving away free tickets for American soldiers to watch him fight.

'I can't win,' Ali said. 'There are some people back home, mostly white folks I have to tell you, who would have me boiled in oil no matter what I say or do. They can't see that it was wrong of us to be bombin' and setting fire to them innocent people in Vietnam. I'd be the first to fight for my country in a just cause, but what we did in 'Nam was wrong, so wrong. Now I'm giving the American Army boys some free entertainment to give them somethin' to cheer out here far away from home, and there are people who are callin' me all the bad names they can put their tongue to for caring about my countrymen. But it don't bother me. Only the judgement of Allah matters and I know I'm doing the right thing.'

Richard Dunn continued training oblivious to all this drama, and at a trial weigh-in at the end of the session he found his weight was 4lb down below the 15st he was aiming for. He was over-trained. Jimmy Devanney gave him a day off, and he went shopping in Munich for a present for Janet.

'Bought her a music box,' he reported. 'She collects them for a hobby, and they all play t'same tune. [He hummed the music for me] De-de-de-dum, dum-de-dum-de-de-dum.'

For those of you who can't read music, he was humming the theme tune from *Dr Zhivago*. But it was Dr Pacheco who was more on my mind. Was Ali really ready for the taking? Had Richard got lucky with his timing?

Could I yet see Jarvis Astaire running naked around Wembley Stadium?

* * *

Another telephone call from Bob Arum, this time to Muhammad Ali. He had just received sky-high extra bills from the two hotels where the helpers, healers, hawkers, hucksters and hangers-on were staying, all of them signing receipts to Ali's room.

They were summoned en masse to an emergency meeting at the Bayerischer Hof hotel, where I took an eavesdropper's place on the periphery of a chandeliered, deep-carpeted room that was used for lectures and corporate announcements. Ali was centre stage in a large armchair like a king on his throne. I was seeing another face of The Greatest, the angry Ali. It was not a pretty sight.

His opening salvo had most of his followers shrinking in their seats. 'Listen up, motherfuckers,' he said, with a cold thread of steel in his world-famous voice, 'I've just been told

I've gotta pay an extra 50,000 bucks because so many of you are taking liberties with food, room service and, most of all, telephone calls back home to the good ol' US of A.'

He picked on the most celebrated of his disciples, Bundini Brown, who worked as his motivator and companion and was responsible for his most imitated catchphrase, 'Float like a butterfly, sting like a bee.'

'You, Bundini, just how many phone calls can you make in a day? How many meals can you eat?'

'Right on, Champ,' wailed a man answering to the name of Jeremiah who used to be a caretaker at a mosque in Philadelphia and was now known as Ali's 'Amen Man'.

Bundini's eyes began filling with tears. 'Why pick on me, Champ? Why pick on ol' Bundini? I done wait on you hand and foot, man.'

'I'm just using you as an example,' Ali explained, clearly wanting to get his message across to everybody; the hustlers selling t-shirts, the shoe-shine boys he'd brought from Louisville, the dodgy watch salesmen, the ticket scalpers who we in the UK would call touts, the kitchen workers, the masseurs, the Muslim preachers and a couple of dozen hangers-on Ali had picked up during his world travels. All of them in Munich at his expense.

The heavyweight champion of the world took his time looking around at the odd-ball gathering, no doubt wondering who half of them were. The one thing they all had in common was that they had flown the Atlantic to Munich on an Ali-paid freebie. Several times he used the 'N' word as a form of expletive, staring hard at each of his followers as if eye-balling them before a fight.

'Listen, I take you all over the world,' he said. 'You see places. You learn things. Never been anywhere in your life. Now you treat me like this.'

'That's right, That's right!' echoed Jeremiah.

'Look, fellas,' Ali said as he started to soften, 'I don't mind you eatin'. You want three steaks for dinner, get three steaks. I don't want anybody goin' hungry. But I don't wantcha wastin' food. Sendin' food back. And as for them telephone calls; you can't be callin' New York and Chicago and LA every minute. I don't mind a man callin' his wife and kids once a day. Five minutes on each call, all right. I knows all about bein' homesick. But those half-hour conversations have gotta stop.'

This was a weary Ali talking. He was tired of the travelling, tired of the training, tired of the circus. Bottom line is he was a lovely, caring man and gullible for any hard-luck story. One of his crowd told me, 'You don't have to be a professional con artist to get anything out of Ali. He's got such a big heart that it's easy to part him from his money, and a lot of people take him to the cleaners.'

His lecture lasted for 20 minutes, and all his hangers-on shuffled out of the room like chastened schoolboys. Ali told me later, 'Nobody has had this kind of crowd around him. Not even Frank Sinatra or Elvis Presley. They rely on me and I won't let them down, but they've gotta be sensible and not take me for a fool.'

Telephone calls to the United States from the two hotels dropped by 80 per cent after the meeting and the food bills shrank as the hangers-on realised they could be losing their meal ticket.

Ali went back to the gymnasium and to promoting his book, appearing on a German daytime television show in which he sparred with five volunteers from the audience, including a middle-aged housewife and a senior citizen. It was all toe-curlingly embarrassing, and if that's the way to sell books then count me out.

Meantime, Richard Dunn returned to training and found himself being jeered and booed by spectators as he sparred with Neville Meade and Eddie Fenton and slogged the punchbag.

Ali's hangers-on had found a way to serve their master.

We were joined by a team of Puma representatives who had signed Richard to an exclusive deal to wear their sportswear. He was getting a £10,000 fee, much more than he had earned in 95 per cent of his fights.

This made a story in the German newspapers because it meant an escalation of the sales war between Puma and Adidas. They were both German sportswear companies launched by brothers Adi and Rudi Dassler in the 1940s, disbanding their joint family business to start global brands in rivalry to each other.

Ali famously wore white Adidas boots with the twirling red laces, and American Everlast shorts. Richard was Puma from head to toe, with the leaping Puma logo on his dressing gown and shorts, all designed in the claret and blue colour of his parachute regiment.

When Ali got to hear that Dunn would be wearing his parachute colours, he said, 'I wish him a happy landing when he hits that canvas.'

I wrote a response from Richard, 'Ali will be my fall guy.' Yes, I had sold my soul.

Now we prepared to welcome Romark.

Round Seven

'You are doomed, Ali – doomed.'

ROMARK ARRIVED two days ahead of the fight, by which time Richard had gone into his shell as the enormity of the task ahead started to gnaw at him. What nobody had told me is that since his altercation with Malcolm Allison, Romark had suffered a facial stroke that had left his face contorted, with one eye slightly higher than the other. Not a pretty sight. It was Mickey who nicknamed him 'Eyesiah'.

He had distinctive eyes that swivelled and you got the sense he had peripheral vision. To say the least, he left a disturbing first impression. Remember that great British comedian Marty Feldman, with the bulbous eyes, the star of *Young Frankenstein*? Then you have a picture in your head of the Romark who joined us in Munich.

A man of around 50 with a receding hairline that suggested his mental powers did not stretch to saving his locks, Romark oozed an air of confidence and breezed into our small group as if he were the cavalry coming to save the day. He knew from all the leaked stories that the show was in trouble, and he saw it as Romark to the rescue. Little did any of us know that he had a secret agenda.

With the help of the *Daily Mirror*, we had brought him over to Munich to try to hypnotise Richard Dunn into causing the boxing upset of the century by defeating arguably the greatest fighter ever to climb through the ropes. But, without a word to anybody, Romark had decided he had a bigger mountain to conquer. His sights, a little on the wonky side, were set on the big man himself, Muhammad Ali.

On his first evening eating with the Dunn party in the hotel restaurant he regaled us with tales of the unexpected from his wide-ranging career, during which he claimed to have hypnotised presidents, kings and queens. I quickly came to the conclusion that you took everything he said and divided it by ten to get somewhere near the truth of what he was claiming. He told us that he now had a Harley Street practice after starting out as an actor, and later discovering that he had what he described as 'extraordinary mental strength'. 'I can overcome any problem big or small by using my mind energy,' he said. 'Even recently when I had my stroke, I cured myself without need of hospitals or doctors. It's all in the mind. Positivity breeds posterity.'

I wasn't going to be the one to say he was talking out of his posterior.

One of Romark's stories was that while working in Africa, he had been attacked by a lion and had hypnotised it as it went for the kill. He admitted there were no witnesses but that a safari ranger who arrived seconds later swore that he found the lion asleep at Romark's feet. Another classic was that he hypnotised an entire TV audience into giving up smoking in the days when he had his own BBC television show. The fact that the show did not make it to a second series suggested that the BBC found him out. No smoke without fire.

He detected my scepticism. 'Norman, I get bad vibes from you,' he said, suddenly becoming Sherlock Holmes. 'What do I have to do to convince you that I am the genuine article?'

Richard Dunn intervened. 'Hypnotise our Norm,' he challenged. 'Let's see you put action where your mouth is.'

Romark shook his head. 'No, he is too hostile,' he said, as if selecting a jury. 'My subjects have to be willing to be put under the influence. I cannot overcome the negative field between us.'

I said that I would clear my mind and bury my disbelief, and I made an honest attempt to dismiss my doubts. I had considered all magicians and so-called mentalists as con men ever since I had worked as scriptwriter on a TV pilot in which every trick involved a relative of the featured illusionist.

This moment of truth in Munich was in my drinking days (I have been dry since 1978) and after several Drambuies I was relaxed and ready for Romark.

'I want you to look into my eyes,' he said, which gave me a fit of the giggles because it was like trying to stare into the window of a slot machine. Romark got irritable. 'You either give me your full attention,' he snapped, 'or we forget it. I can only work with cooperative people. Nobody can be hypnotised against their will.'

Finally I controlled myself and went along with his instructions. 'Relax and look into my eyes; when I snap my fingers you will drift into a sleep.' The next five or so minutes are a complete blank, and I was later told by witnesses George Biddles and Mickey Duff that I went out like a light and into a trance.

'Unless you were acting,' the equally sceptical Mickey said, 'he had you out quicker than a left hook from Joe Louis.'

George Biddles nodded, 'You definitely looked out of it. I was cynical but then honestly believed that he'd hypnotised you.'

While I was drifting off, Romark apparently said to me, 'When I snap my fingers, you will wake up and be convinced your fists are made of iron.' The next I knew I was banging on the dining table, and the knives and forks were jumping in the air. I really did think my fists were made of iron.

Romark then told me that when he next snapped his fingers I would slowly come out of my sleep and that my hands would feel as normal.

I am not making this up, and as I emerged from my trance I had memories of all that had happened but as if I was seeing it as an out-of-body experience.

Suddenly I saw Romark in a new light. Perhaps my first impression of him being a crank and a con man was wrong. Now if he could convince Richard to think that *his* fists were made of iron, that would quite literally be hard for Ali to take.

He went off with Richard, Jimmy and George Biddles to a private room for the promised *Daily Mirror* exclusive photograph. The next morning they featured a front-page picture story showing Romark performing the same levitation illusion with which he had impressed Southampton manager Lawrie McMenemy. The photo featured Richard sitting on a local fraulein who appeared to be suspended in mid-air, with Biddles and Devanney looking on and Romark beaming in the background.

'I know it's a bloody trick,' Richard told me, 'but I had to admit I were flabbergasted by it.'

So now the four million *Mirror* readers knew that Romark was going to hypnotise Dunn before the big fight.

Jarvis Astaire was delighted with the publicity and reported a spike in ticket sales for his closed-circuit theatres and cinemas. Job done.

* * *

Noon the next day, Monday, 24 May, was weigh-in day for the early hours Tuesday fight. The scales had been set up on a temporary stage at the Circus-Krone building, a five-minute car ride away from the Munich Hilton. This was, fittingly, one of the most famous indoor circus venues in the world. It tied in nicely with what had so far been a circus of a promotion. And there were more send-in-the-clowns moments to come.

Mickey and I decided we would stroll to the weigh-in and invited Romark to come with us. As we walked along the Hilton corridor, who should be coming towards us but Muhammad Ali and his trainer Angelo Dundee? We had a good chuckle and exchanged handshakes. I was about to introduce Romark to the two of them when he suddenly pushed past me and leapt up in front of Ali.

Six inches shorter than the 6ft 3in champion, he said with as wide a stare as he could muster, 'You are doomed to defeat tonight. D-o-o-m-e-d. I'm putting a curse on you.'

Ali fell to his knees laughing uncontrollably, while Dundee asked, 'Who is this nutter?'

'He's our secret weapon,' I said, trying hard to keep a straight face – something beyond the powers of the stroke-stricken Romark. We then continued on our separate ways, with Mickey saying, 'See you at the weigh-in.'

It had to be one of the strangest fight-day confrontations in history, and things got even stranger.

Romark was really buzzing over what he considered his triumph over Ali. 'I've got him worried,' he said. 'He's going to start thinking about that curse I've put on him and it will gradually drain him of confidence.'

'But he was pissing himself laughing,' Mickey pointed out with his usual grace. 'He just thought you were crazy.'

'That's what Malcolm Allison thought. I'll have the last laugh.' Mickey and I shared raised-eyebrow looks.

* * *

When we got to the Circus-Krone it was bedlam, with most of Ali's entourage milling around on the temporary stage. Their behaviour was appalling and they had become an embarrassment to the champion, but he was too easy-going and accommodating to say anything to them. I cannot think of any other sports personality or showbiz celebrity in history who has had their fans feeding off them to anything like the same extent.

His manager Herbert Muhammad reckoned that the hangers-on cost Ali an average $50,000 per fight from when he first became champion, and in Munich the bill was nearer $100,000.

An army of singing and chanting Yorkshiremen and paratroopers drowned out Ali's followers at the weigh-in when Richard, wearing just blue y-front pants, scaled a lighter than expected 14st 11lb (207lb). Chewing a strip of Wrigley's gum, Richard acknowledged his vociferous supporters with raised, heavily tattooed arms and then pushed his way through the mob on the stage and put on his distinctive Puma tracksuit.

Next up Ali, wearing his traditional Everlast white shorts and bare-footed. He hit the scales at 15st 10lb, a weight advantage of almost a stone but, more significant, 10lb lighter than against Jimmy Young in April, when he was considered to have given the worst performance of his career.

American PR guru Bobby Goodman turned to me and said, 'That's bad news for your man. Ali has got himself into shape for this defence.'

The words were hardly out of his mouth when there were a series of cracks like rifle shots. The stage on which the weigh-in was being held was collapsing under the tonnage of Ali, his huge sparring partners and the army of hangers-on. There were yells and screams as people were pitched into a sudden hole that had appeared at the heart of the stage.

Ali was the coolest man in the cauldron, and was signalling like a traffic cop to direct people where to position themselves to avoid being crushed.

The stage was gradually cleared and the champion was loudly cheered as he stepped unharmed from the debris. Half a dozen people were treated for minor injuries.

In the far corner of the Circus-Krone, Romark meaningfully double-tapped the side of his nose to suggest that he had something to do with it. He claimed his curse was starting to work.

It all left me feeling in a trance.

Round Eight

'Once upon a time'

WE RETURNED to the Hilton to while away the 11 hours before we needed to leave for the stadium and the fight. This is always a torturous time for the boxers, and Richard was in uncharacteristic grumpy mood. 'Told yer I were over-training,' he said to father-in-law Jimmy Devanney, as he tried to relax in their luxury suite. 'Plan were to come in at 15 stone. Only a bloody half stone out. And Ali's got rid of all that fat he were carrying against Young.'

Manager George Biddles had spent years handling the pre-fight nerves and morose moods of his boxers and had learned to say nowt but nod in agreement with them.

'Just take it easy, Richard lad,' he said, like a headmaster talking to a pupil. 'Your weight is fine. You've never been fitter in your life. Ali has shifted his extra pounds too quickly. Bet he did it with pills rather than exercise.'

He let that sink into Richard's mind, a possibility about which we had all been quietly conjecturing. From being his heaviest and most ponderous ever against Jimmy Young at 230lb in Maryland on 30 April 1976, Ali was now, just 25 days later, down to an almost sleek 220lb, and this while he was on a hectic schedule jetting around the world publicising his autobiography for which he received a $250,000 advance. The book was already into its third reprint less than six months after publication. Ah, the Promised Land.

There were rumours that since his arrival in Munich, Ali had not been training properly, but I knew that to be untrue. It was simply that he continued on American time and, while Germany slept, he worked flat out in the gymnasium.

Biddles dipped back into the past to motivate Richard. 'There was a boxer in the 1930s called James J. Braddock who came off the dole queue to take the world heavyweight title from Max Baer,' he recalled. 'I was a young manager in Leicester at the time and always used him as an example to my boxers as to what could be achieved with the right attitude of mind. The critics didn't give him a prayer, but he got himself as fit as you are today and he won a famous victory and earned himself the nickname of the Cinderella Man. You can make yourself just as famous and become the modern James J. Braddock.'

As Richard tried to imagine what it would be like to go home as the heavyweight champion of the world, Devanney changed the subject to take his mind off the fight. 'No wonder stage bloody collapsed at t'weigh-in just now,' he said, shaking his head in disgust. 'Ali's got more hangers-on than Geoff Boycott's cat's got bloody fleas. Parasites, the lot of them. What t'hell were they doing being allowed on t'stage? Could have got us all killed.'

'Shambolic,' agreed Mickey Duff. 'Never seen anything like it. So much for German efficiency. They're the ones who forgot to plan for a Russian winter. Forgot to allow for extra people on the stage. Thank goodness nobody was seriously injured, but it could have been a disaster.'

A queue of people who had come over from Yorkshire on the charter flights – friends, relatives and committed fans – visited Richard to wish him luck, all of them talking in hushed tones as if paying respects at a funeral parlour. Biddles realised they were making his increasingly nervous boxer agitated rather than building his confidence. He eventually banned everybody from visiting, and our now shrunken group sat quietly making small talk as the clocks suddenly slowed down and minutes started to go by like hours.

Romark joined us, looking buoyant and his bulbous eyes sparkling. 'Well, I've done Ali,' he said. 'Now for King Richard.'

Richard shot him a startled look. 'What you on about? We did the levitating malarkey yesterday.'

'I'm here to hypnotise *you*,' Romark announced, like a surgeon talking to his patient before an operation.

'That were just for publicity,' Richard said. 'Norman's potty idea.'

'Not going to sell tickets now,' Mickey said, veteran of a thousand fight nights. 'Too late for extra bums on seats.'

George Biddles took the floor. 'Look Richard,' he said in the tone of an old, world-weary barrister, 'I've been around this game a long, long time and the way I see it we should try anything we can to get the better of Ali, who let's face it is a phenomenal boxer. We would be deceiving ourselves if we thought anything else.'

'True,' said Mickey. 'Doesn't call himself The Greatest for nothing.'

Devanney threw Mickey a vicious look that was interpreted as 'stop knocking my boy's confidence'.

Biddles continued with his summing up, 'What I feel is that as we have Romark here we should use him. He's convinced he can hypnotise you into beating Ali. Let's give it a go.'

Richard thought long and hard before shrugging his wide shoulders. 'What's to lose? OK, Romark, I'm all yours. Be gentle with me.'

He released an empty laugh, clearly not taking it seriously.

Mickey broke the tension that had invaded the room. 'Hey, have I got a joke for you,' he said, which was always his precursor for the corniest jokes you'll ever hear. We braced ourselves.

'A group of chess fanatics checked into a New York hotel,' he told us, as if sharing a state secret, 'and they stood together in the lobby discussing their recent tournament performances.

'After about an hour, the manager came from behind the reception desk and asked them to leave the lobby. "But why?" the chess players asked. "We're not doing any harm." The manager told them, "Because I can't stand chess nuts boasting in an open foyer."'

The punchline was greeted with groans from Mickey's audience, and Richard said, 'Bloody hell, Romark, put me to sleep.'

It achieved Mickey's aim of easing the intense atmosphere as fight time approached, very slowly. Like chestnuts roasting on an open fire.

* * *

It was after a room service waiter had brought us each a light salad lunch that Romark and Richard disappeared together into the championship challenger's bedroom, and I went off to prepare the press packs that I made available for the score of British pressmen reporting the fight.

They included full fact files on each boxer and, something I did not want Richard to see, my interview with Ali in which he said exactly what he expected to do to the Brit.

It was all typed on my Remington portable and photocopied in the Hilton management office, and then placed in folders for each of the pampered press boys. I wish I'd received the same spoon-fed service in my reporting days!

This is what Ali had told me for British media consumption in our sit-down talk during his break in training at the gymnasium:

'I've seen film of Richard Dunn and he's a good, strong fighter, but certainly not better nor stronger than the likes of George Foreman, Joe Frazier and the big bear Sonny Liston. If I can see them off, why should I have any fear of your Richard Dunn? Are you gonna tell me he's better and stronger than them?

'He has proved himself the best fighter in the whole of Europe. Well I'm the greatest fighter in the whole of the world and I can tell you that he has no right to be in the same town let alone the same ring as me.

'I always like to give my opponents names, just to put them in their place. Let it be known that I've given your Richard the title of Frankenstein and his little trainer guy is Igor. Well, I'm gonna frighten the hell out of them, and they'll have to put that monster back together again when I've finished with him.

'I've done a deal with Dunn that after I've annihilated him he will give me a lifetime's supply of Yorkshire pudding. My ma will welcome that. She's the best cook on the planet.

'I'm told Richard jumps out of planes as a parachutist. Well he'd better wear a parachute in Munich, because I'm gonna give him the heaviest drop of his life. I suggest he learns some German, "Acht, neun, zehn, aus!"

'I have a poem for him:

Richard Dunn, you might fall in one
Or maybe a few rounds later
But I promise you it'll be no fun
As I eat you alive like an alligator

'Tell all my British fans that I appreciate their support, and I apologise for what I'm going to do to their man. Nothin' personal. It's business. Say goodnight, Dick.'

'Say goodnight, Dick,' was the popular sign-off note on the hugely popular *Rowan & Martin's Laugh-In* TV series.

I had the folders hand-delivered to each of the journalists in their various hotels and the interpretation I liked best was by *The Guardian*'s witty, waspish Frank Keating:

'Tonight in the Boxhalle, Munich, Muhammad Ali, of the United States of America and The Universe, will defend his world heavyweight title against Richard Dunn, of 23 Railway Cuttings, Bradford, West Yorkshire.'

I would give my left testicle to be able to write an intro like that (which is devalued, incidentally, following a vasectomy in 1970).

Having done my publicist's duties I then returned to Richard's suite of rooms to see how he had fared with Romark. It was after ten o'clock and Biddles had dismissed the hypnotist. 'He was getting on our nerves,' the crotchety old manager told me. 'I've told him we'll see him after the fight.'

Mickey had left to go to the stadium and it was 10.15pm when a yawning Richard emerged from his bedroom. You could almost sense him wishing the fight had been and gone. I waited for him to get orientated before asking him how he had got on with Romark.

'I lay on t'bed in my tracksuit,' he said, 'and he started telling me a bedtime story as if I were a kid. He then gave me t'same treatment he gave you last night. Said I should relax and look into his eyes. I had to bite my tongue to stop meself from laughing. He started saying, "Once upon a time there was a handsome prince," and clicked his fingers. I pretended to go to sleep and he went on about the Prince meeting Cinderella.'

He paused and shook his head, wondering if he was dreaming. 'Suddenly said that when he snapped his fingers again I'd wake up convinced my fists have been turned to iron. I didn't want to hurt his feelings by telling him that I thought it were all rubbish. So I played along with him, then I went into a proper sleep. Next I knew Jimmy were shaking me awake to tell me it were time to go t'stadium.'

The $64,000 question, 'And how do your fists feel?' I found myself asking.

'Ali's going to find out very soon,' Richard said with unexpected determination, 'when I land on his chin.'

There was a hilarious interlude when the Puma representatives arrived with the 'go-to-work' clothes for the big fight that would give their brand televised promotion right across the United States and in closed-circuit cinemas throughout the United Kingdom. Richard elected to put his on at the stadium, while cornermen George and Jimmy decided to try theirs on before taking the ten-minute limousine drive to the Olympiahalle.

When they came out of their respective bedrooms dressed for action, Richard nearly fell off his chair laughing. Both were in the same claret and blue parachute regiment colours as Dunn, but the difference was the sweaters were sparkling with diamante that would have looked at home on Liberace.

'You look like t'bloody Four Tops,' said Richard. 'Where's t'other two?' Devanney was going to be the man in the ring working with the challenger, so he was contracted by Puma to wear the over-the-top gear. Biddles, embarrassed by his pop star appearance, announced that as he was going to be standing on the apron outside the ring he, to quote George, 'did not have to make a clown of myself'.

He went back into the bedroom and changed into the cream cardigan that he had worn the night Richard shocked Bernd August to earn this fight with Muhammad Ali. 'It's my lucky top,' he told the protesting Puma team.

We all knew that Richard would need all the luck he could get.

Round Nine

Dressing-room blackout

JUST FOUR years earlier the then spanking-new Olympiahalle had been home to the 1972 Olympic gymnastics, when a waif of a Russian girl called Olga Korbut wowed the world with her balletic acrobatics. Now it was the venue for Muhammad Ali's latest defence of his world heavyweight championship and I was with the challenger Richard Dunn as he entered the near-empty stadium three hours ahead of the 3am fight time.

Manager George Biddles led our small party into the main entrance, followed by trainer and father-in-law Jimmy 'Pop' Devanney, his two likeable, fresh-faced young professional boxer sons Jimmy junior and Lawrence, an increasingly anxious Richard and me, carrying my portable typewriter ready to cover the fight for those British newspapers not represented at the ringside.

None of us were sure of the way to the dressing rooms and Biddles pushed open a door signposted 'Ausgang'. This, of course, was an exit and we found ourselves face to face with the 4th Paras enthusiastically rehearsing how they were going to lead Richard into the ring.

'Dickie, Dickie, Dickie,' they chanted the second they saw their hero, who gave an embarrassed wave and then darted back into the arena. 'This is fucking amateur night out,' he complained, as he struggled to control his nerves and emotions with fight night now a reality. You could see it dawning on him that he was about to climb into the ring with arguably the greatest heavyweight boxer of all time. Rather him than me.

'It's OK, son, found it,' 'Pop' said, pointing towards the signpost that read 'Eingang Die Umkleidekabine'. I was about to compliment Jimmy on his German when I saw beneath it in English, 'Dressing rooms'.

Richard's dressing room was about the size of a squash court, with a huge star on the door and beneath it a poster announcing the fight and 'Richard Dunn' in huge gothic lettering on white cardboard glued to the wooden panelling.

An NBC crewman holding a revolutionary portable camera with a long, snaking lead appeared from nowhere and followed Richard into the dressing room then took up a position in the far corner, focusing in on Richard as he sat himself down on a black leather chair.

Jimmy Devanney gave the cameraman a double take, before demanding, 'What the fuck are you doing here?'

'I'll be here the whole night, my friend,' the cameraman said in a made-in-America drawl.

'Like fuck you will not my friend,' Devanney said, suddenly pushing the TV man towards the 'ausgang' door.

George Biddles intervened. 'It's in the contract, Jim,' he said. 'They're giving it total coverage in the States.'

'Not in OUR dressing room they're not,' he said, now in the grip of uncontrolled anger. 'I want this to be private for Dickie.' He continued to push the protesting cameraman towards the door, and then with a sudden moment of inspiration he switched off the dressing room lights. 'That'll stop you,' he said, in a triumphant tone.

It rather backfired on Jim when a TV monitor up on a ledge in the dressing room flickered into life, and there was Muhammad Ali doing a promo for the fight from *his* room on the opposite side of the arena. 'Take your seats, folks, for another great NBC fight night,' he told viewers across the US. 'I'm being challenged by a Brit who is the champion of all of Europe. Watch me knocking him to the canvas like tea into the Boston Harbour. Watch it right here on NBC; your eyes won't believe what they're about to see.'

Richard sat there staring at the screen, wondering if he was dreaming it all. If so, it had turned into a nightmare.

* * *

With the first of the supporting contests under way, Mickey Duff tracked me down in Richard's now orderly, camera-free dressing room. 'Have I got news for you,' he said, with the boyish enthusiasm he always showed when he had information to share. 'I've had a word with Ali and he's agreed to let me have his gloves at the end of the fight. We've got a show later this week at the Anglo-American, where we're raising funds for Chris Finnegan [whose career had just been finished by a detached retina].'

He then told me the part I would play in the glove story. 'As soon as the fight's over,' he said, 'I'll climb into the ring and as Angelo pulls them off he'll hand them to me. You be close by Ali's corner and I will pass them down to you for safe keeping. It'll be bedlam in the ring. Always is after an Ali fight. The Champ has agreed to sign the gloves when you take them to his room at the Hilton two hours after the fight has finished. He'll be expecting you.'

'Which room number?' I asked fairly reasonably. 'I thought Ali was staying at the Bayerischer Hof hotel with the rest of his entourage.'

Mickey laughed. 'He's not *that* dumb,' he said. 'With that crowd he'd never get any rest. He's been sleeping at the Hilton during the daytime. Ali always operates to American time zones. He's an expert at it. No matter where he is in the world, he gets his kip at the right time to suit his body clock.'

'And the room number is?' I asked again.

Mickey shrugged. 'I'll get it for you,' he said, matter-of-fact. 'The important thing is we get those gloves. They'll fetch several thousand at auction, provided we've got Ali's signature on them.'

I was not going to say the same to Mickey that I'd said to Jarvis Astaire, 'What if Richard Dunn wins?' The thought of Mickey running naked around Wembley Stadium was too much to contemplate.

* * *

George Biddles had made it clear he wanted the dressing room empty an hour before the fight, with only a resting Richard, trainer Devanney and himself inside. There were 60 minutes to go when I called in to wish Richard luck. I had grown enormously fond of the big man, who was far brighter than people realised. Between them, he and Pop had continually amazed me with their wide breadth of knowledge.

Richard was sucking in great gulps of air when I bent forward to shake his right hand, his left one being bandaged by the caring, conscientious Jimmy. He had just made his sixth visit to the toilet in an hour and the colour had drained from his pugnacious face. The challenger was like a man about to face the electric chair.

'Good luck, mate,' I said in my Cockney tones that Richard had always found amusing. 'Just remember the whole of Yorkshire is behind you. There's not a fitter man in the world than you. Give it real welly.'

He gulped as he tried to smile, and was clearly close to being physically sick. I had often been around boxers before they went into battle, and fear was the common denominator. Richard was frightened to death.

'Just remember your regiment's motto,' I said, with words that I had rehearsed for this moment. 'Ready For Everything.'

Richard repeated it, but in its Latin form, 'Ultriqie Paratis'.

I leant forward and kissed the lovely big man on his cheek. 'Give over you big pillock,' he said, choking on his words.

You could have cut the emotion with a knife.

As I prepared to leave him for his final preparations, I said, 'Remember, Richard, you've got fists of iron.'

I left him laughing.

* * *

A little aside about the 'sport' of boxing and why I have torn feelings about it. For me it is one of the greatest of all measures of men's courage and character. Just climbing through the ropes is a victory. But I know that it is a bonkers 'sport' that should be banned, which makes me a king-size hypocrite for taking money to encourage people to go and watch it.

I am talking as an ex-publicist with a troubled conscience. The people I detest most of all are those spectators who demand more and more and criticise referees for stopping fights. Of course, it takes a lot of courage to sit and cheer and jeer. So many of the boxers I used to write about and represent as a publicist are either 'up there' or do not know their name. As for women boxing, the thought of middle-aged ladies wandering around punch drunk depresses the life out of me.

Richard himself paid the price for all the punches he took and suffered from dementia before reaching old age. It is brutal and barbaric. But I have to confess I've had a lifetime's love of it and am continually drawn to watch it like an alcoholic to a drink. And I could bore you all day on the history of the sport. Now back to our story of the man who put a curse on Muhammad Ali.

* * *

As I left Richard behind in the dressing room after our emotional conversation, I bumped into Romark wandering like a lost soul. 'Have you got a seat?' I asked.

'Yes,' he said, 'with the *Mirror* boys. How's Richard? They won't let me in to see him.'

'He's ready for battle,' I said, not mentioning that he was in the grip of fear. 'He is determined to give it his all.'

'I've done all I can,' he said, really thinking that he'd had an effect on both boxers. Ali dismissed him as a nut. Richard just ignored him.

'It will be fascinating to see the outcome,' I commented, trying to think of an escape route. He could talk for Britain.

I was rescued by Mickey returning to tell me the number of the champion's suite. He was in boisterous mood, and felt he could now tell Romark exactly what he thought of him.

'Mr Markham,' he said, no holds barred, 'I think you're a charlatan. All that bullshit about being able to hypnotise sportsmen. You've got as much genuine power as a flat battery.'

'Ah, a sceptic,' said Romark, a huge understatement from an angry man who – like Mickey – was spoiling for a fight. He was pissed off at not having been allowed to see Richard in the dressing room.

'Not a sceptic,' Mickey said, 'a realist with my eyes wide open. You deal in mumbo jumbo. I used to work the markets and know all about the mind tricks people can play, but to try to pass it off as some sort of God-given gift is fraud of the worst kind.'

Romark's eyes were bulging out of his head, and I was concerned that he was going to have another stroke.

'Hypnosis is a well-studied and legitimate form of adjunct treatment for many conditions,' he said. 'I can point to hundreds of cases where I have been able to pass on my mental strength to make people perform to their potential, even surpass it.'

'I'm a gambling man,' Mickey said, 'and I'm happy to give you odds of 20 to one that your hypnosis of Richard Dunn is as phoney as a nine-bob note. I'll bet ten grand that Ali will beat him inside the distance and give you £200,000 if Dunn becomes heavyweight champion of the world.'

'Well I'm *not* a gambling man,' Romark replied, 'and even if I were I would not take your bet because I was not allowed to finish my work with Richard. I was expecting to be invited into the dressing room to give him one last session. I just hope that my afternoon influence has not worn off.' Mickey held his arms out, palms of hands upwards and open as if preparing for prayer. 'Making your excuses already,' he mocked. 'If anybody's got mental strength it's Muhammad Ali. You claim to have put a spell on him. Well, he's put a spell on most of his opponents with a combination of his punches and psychology. Nothing fake about the champion.'

Romark slunk away, mumbling unintelligibly to himself, and Mickey laughed. 'Reckon he's trying self-hypnosis.'

He looked knowingly around at an arena not half full, like a sommelier testing the wine. 'The schmucks wouldn't listen to me,' he said. 'The second that Dunn stopped August I said the fight should be switched to Yorkshire. Nearly everybody you can see here who's not from Yorkshire is watching for free with tickets supplied by Ali. It's madness.'

Sydney Hulls, a dear old friend and former colleague from the *Daily Express*, joined us ready to report on the fight. His father, also Sydney Hulls, had been Britain's top boxing promoter in the 1930s.

'I'm here to report on another horizontal British heavyweight,' the lovely old cynic said to me and Mickey. 'Last time I was here was to report on Olga Korbut doing all sorts of somersaults. Tonight it will be Dunn spreadeagled on the floor and getting a ten ...'

It was going to be a long night. My heart was with Richard. My head was saying Ali.

Round Ten

The fight

THERE IS no sports event that quite matches a world heavyweight title fight for generating tension and excitement in the build-up to the action. Even in a half-full (or half-empty) arena, I had a gut-wrenching sensation as the contestants approached the ring, first Richard marching proudly behind a posse of his parachuting pals holding a huge Union Jack stretched above their heads. Then the majestic Ali, bouncing in a rhythmic walk to the ring as he if owned it (which he soon would).

The entries were more gladiatorial than the all-singing and dancing extravaganzas promoters put on today, when it sometimes takes longer for the boxers to get into the ring than for them to fight. Please, Messrs Hearn, Warren et al, note: less is more. Jack Solomons used to do it with a single spotlight and a trumpet fanfare, and that would make the hair on the back of your neck stand on end. But back to the fight.

As I sat typing on my Remington portable, my hands were as clammy as if I had put them in a bowl of water. I was desperate for Richard to do himself justice, while knowing that he was out of his class against a man who had continually shown he was The Greatest by deed as well as word.

There had been signs that Ali was on the downhill run, but did Richard have sufficient ambition and ammunition to send him slipping and sliding to one of the shock defeats of the century?

This is how I captured it round by round, typing just a row back from the ringside and with such a close-up view that I could almost feel as well as see and hear the punches. My running report, much of it in the present tense, was relayed back to the ViewSport head office and circulated by fax to newspapers that were not represented in the full-to-capacity press seats. Muhammad Ali was in town and no self-respecting sportswriter wanted to miss it:

'Champion Muhammad Ali and challenger Richard Dunn have had to stand through three national anthems, first the West German version, followed by "God Save the Queen" heartily sung by the 3,000 Richard Dunn supporters who have made the trip to Munich, and finally the "Star Spangled Banner", with Ali noticeably not singing a note before spinning round and saying a Muslim prayer while standing in a corner with his back to Dunn.

'Support in the Olympiahalle is overwhelmingly for the champion, mainly because he gave away thousands of tickets to Munich-based US soldiers to save a show that was very nearly cancelled due to lack of interest from German fight fans. This is his seventh defence of his WBA and WBC heavyweight crowns.

'Dunn won the right to this title challenge by stopping 6ft 7in German champion Bernd August in three rounds in a championship eliminator at the Royal Albert Hall in April. He is a sandy-haired 6ft 4in Yorkshireman, a rugged southpaw, scaffolder and parachuting soldier, who has made 67 drops. Ali has promised to make it 68 tonight!

'There has been a lot of conjecture about Ali's weight and whether he was training properly for this fight, particularly following an unimpressive and disputed points victory over Jimmy Young in his last title defence in Maryland on 30 April. He was then a sluggish, heaviest-ever 230lb. Amazingly he has shed 10lb and looks relatively sleek as he and Dunn are called to the centre of the ring for final instructions from German referee Herbert Tomser. Chief second Angelo Dundee is at Ali's side and Dunn is accompanied by veteran manager George Biddles and his trainer and father-in-law, Jimmy Devanney. But as the first bell rings Dunn and Ali stand alone, Richard suddenly looking like an orphan in an approaching storm.

'**ROUND 1:** Dunn, who had been looking apprehensive during the national anthems, has clearly made up his mind to "give it a go". He attacks Ali in the opening seconds and bounces a southpaw right off the champion's chin, but Ali was dancing backwards and he rides the punch. Dunn attacks again, this time with both fists but Ali backs on to the ropes and lands a left-right counter that forces the challenger to take his first reverse-gear step. Dunn is surprising everybody, particularly Ali, with the ferocity of his assaults and the champion takes two head shots that convinces him he needs to put Dunn in his place, and he throws a right uppercut that jolts the Yorkshireman. Again, Dunn comes forward and Ali retreats to the ropes just as he did in his famous Rumble in the Jungle with George Foreman. Could this be Mutiny in Munich by Dunn, who is being cheered on by a platoon of his parachute pals?

'In the final moments of a hectic, breathtaking first round Ali reminds the challenger who's boss with a left-right combination that stops the charging Bradford Bull in his tracks. But the determined challenger is back on his forward march as the bell signals the end of round one. Just Dunn's round.

'Leading international matchmaker Mickey Duff is alongside me and says, "I cannot believe it. Dunn is fighting like a man possessed. He definitely had Ali rattled a couple of times in that first round. The champion knows he has got to start taking this seriously."

'**ROUND 2:** The challenger comes out full of fire and determination, and Ali has to get up on his toes and dance his way out of range of the British boy's tattoo of powerful right jabs. The Dunn supporters are cheering themselves hoarse and making it sound as if there is a capacity crowd in the half-full Olympiahalle. This is where Russia's lithe and lovely Olga Korbut thrilled the crowds with her gymnastics artistry in the 1972 Olympics. Now it is Richard Dunn who is providing the thrills, not with Olga's grace but with his own brand of assault and battery. He said before the fight that he is going to give Ali the fright of his life and he has certainly surprised the champion with his energy and the power of his punches.

'Ali is now starting to plant his feet and putting extra power into his right hand bombs, traditionally the best way to unsettle a southpaw. Dunn takes a right cross to the jaw and then, instantly, a second one as Ali lets loose with venom. They said Dunn had a suspect jaw but he has taken both punches well and is being aggressive again after stealing a breather in a clinch. Ali said before the fight that he would be dancin' and jabbin', but he is having to change his plan and has got himself into a war. Moments before the end of this second session, the champion is clubbed to the head by a southpaw swing and the look of surprise on his face translates as, "This is tougher than I expected." Again, narrowly Dunn's round.

'Mickey Duff, who has been screaming encouragement and advice to Dunn from his perch close to the ring apron, comments, "This is as good as I've ever seen Dunn fight. I honestly didn't think he had a chance, but he has unquestionably got Ali concerned. I'm astonished. But there's a long way to go. Ali has been here many times, and knows just how to pace himself."

'Ringside seats that are usually the reserve of the rich and famous at world heavyweight title fights, have been largely taken over by GIs. Ali gave them the best seats in the house. "Geez," said one in my hearing, "looks like we could be here to see the end of Ali. The Brit is giving him a helluva fight." The TV microphones pick up that both George Biddles and "Pop" Devanney are willing Richard on, telling him he is producing the fight of his life. "Doing yourself proud, lad," says the venerable Biddles, almost unable to believe his eyes. Dare he start to think that he could be managing the heavyweight champion of the world? George Biddles is from Leicestershire and a manager for 50 years.

'"Keep him on t'back foot, son," Devanney urges. "Force him to t'ropes and knock ten skittles out of him. This is your night."

'**ROUND 3:** Ali dances backwards for a full minute, taunting Dunn and saying, "This the best you got, sucker?" The Yorkshireman, inspired by his chanting, cheering countrymen, rushes the champion to his own corner and Ali has to cover up to block a fusillade of punches from the stoked-up challenger. The 20ft square ring has been reduced to the size of a London telephone box as they trade punches on the ropes directly above me. Then Ali turns Dunn and is away like a getaway driver on a bank raid, back-pedalling around the ring with his old "float like a butterfly, sting like a bee" rhythm and zing.

'In the second half of the round, Ali changes tactics and stops running. He makes it clear he is prepared to slug it out with Dunn and they each score with hooks and jabs as they swap full-blooded punches in the centre of the ring. It has developed into a full-out war and the spectators are on the edge of their seats or standing and screaming in near hysteria.

'NBC producers will be in raptures because this is making for great television coverage of a fight that few people really wanted.

'Richard Dunn is exceeding everybody's expectations and at the end of three rounds most good judges have him slightly ahead on points. But there are still 12 rounds to go. At the pulsating pace they have set, it will never last the distance. Angelo Dundee and Bundini Brown are in harmony, shouting from the corner, "Keep moving to your left, Champ, to your left." Dunn has a slight cut high on his forehead as the round finishes and as "Pop" Devanney cleans it up manager Biddles tells Richard, "Beautiful, lad, you're boxing beautifully. Can you keep it up?" Dunn, breathing heavily, responds, "I'm givin' good as I'm getting. He knows I'm in there with him." An understatement if ever there was one, because Ali is having to reach down into his boots to keep the challenger at bay.

'Mickey Duff is up out of his seat, shouting at Dunn just yards away, "Keep going, Richard. Same come-forward tactics. Don't let him settle."

'Hypnotist Romark, who claims to have confronted BOTH boxers before the fight, is jumping up and down with excitement in the press seats where he is a guest of the *Daily Mirror*. He is heard shouting towards Dunn, "Remember you've got fists of iron, Richard. Fists of iron."

'**ROUND 4:** Dunn comes hurrying out to the centre of the ring at the start of the fourth round ready to continue harassing and chasing Ali, but now the champion stands his ground. There is a dramatic swing in the fortunes of the fight halfway through the round when Ali catches Dunn with a swift right hand counter to the jaw. It takes a second for the punch to take effect and then the challenger suddenly stumbles to the canvas. Ali is standing over him shouting "Say goodnight, Dick" and the referee interrupts his count while directing the champion to a neutral corner.

'Dunn is shaken but up at six and ready to fight on at eight. He covers up as Ali unleashes a barrage of rights and lefts. One right hand smashes through Dunn's defence and he staggers as if he has walked into an unseen wall. He forces himself forward and tries to cling on to Ali like a drowning man but another salvo of punches drops him to his knees with 25 seconds of the round left. Bravely, madly he pulls himself up at eight and again goes after Ali, who this time drops him briefly to his knees before the bell comes to the rescue.

'It would have been easy for Richard to quit at this point; nobody would have blamed him because he had already gone beyond the call of duty, but he insisted on coming out for the fifth. He always said that he would go out on his shield.

'Ali spent most of the interval measuring out and miming exactly where he was going to drop Dunn and he was shouting, "Parachute drop number 68 coming up." After his early scares, he was now enjoying himself.

'**ROUND 5:** Amazingly, Richard came running out of his corner at the start of the fifth round like a greyhound released from the traps. He drove Ali back to the ropes, even though still in a daze from the battering he had taken in the fourth round. The courageous Yorkshireman was fighting on sheer instinct and landed several desperate blows before Ali sent him to the canvas again with a thunderous right.

'Those who thought it was all over did not understand the fighting spirit of paratrooper Dunn. He was up again and still chasing Ali until what the champion called his straight-from-the-shoulder, right-hand karate punch dropped him for a sixth time just as Dunn's excited supporters were thinking he would survive to the sixth round. Few could believe it when Richard somehow pulled himself up yet again, but as he sank back against the ropes, the referee signalled that was the end. As a concussed Dunn protested that he could carry on, Ali stood windmilling his right hand to show he was ready to administer the knockout blow.

'It was one of the bravest performances ever witnessed from a world heavyweight title challenger. Dunn, battered and bruised, made up for the difference in class with a willpower and tenacity that made him a hero in defeat.'

Ali's personal physician Dr Ferdie Pacheco was alongside me, just having put down his microphone after giving a co-commentary on the fight for NBC viewers. 'Your guy put up an unbelievably brave show,' he said. 'If that had been the Ali who fought so poorly against Jimmy Young three weeks ago he'd have got beaten, but he dug down and found some of the old Ali magic. But I'm going to keep up my mantra.

Enough is enough. Ali is long overdue hanging up those golden gloves of his.'

Incredibly, Richard had the energy and passion left to join a triumphant Ali at the after-fight interview in the crowded ring and asked for a return fight that we all knew would never happen. It was bravado beyond the understanding of we mere mortals. Ali praised his courage and said Richard deserved another shot at the title, and that he was definitely 'a top contender who will come again'.

But the champion had such a crowded calendar that there was as much chance of Dunn getting a second crack at Ali as there was of Jarvis Astaire running naked around Wembley Stadium.

* * *

Ali, whose next 'fight' was scheduled to be a box-wrestling match against Japanese giant Antonio Inoki in Tokyo in June, revealed that he had dismantled Richard with a secret weapon. 'I call it my "accupunch", taught to me by taekwondo grandmaster and one of my special cornermen tonight, Jhoon Rhee. I'm gonna use it on Inoki and tried it out on Richard's chin. You saw the result.'

By now there were more than 50 people in the seething ring, including man with a mission Mickey Duff. He had got his hands on Ali's gloves after a tug of war with an NBC crewman, who had briefly hijacked them from Angelo Dundee.

Mickey passed them to me like precious bars of gold. All I had to do now was to get Ali to sign them. It was one of the stranger assignments of my career.

Round Eleven

Glove story

TWO HOURS after the fight I tapped lightly and politely on the door of suite 77 of the Munich Hilton. In a black Puma holdall I carried the gloves with which Muhammad Ali had just retained his world heavyweight title with a brutal fifth-round stoppage of British bulldog Richard Dunn. I had walked nervously with them through the packed downstairs lobby, where dozens of the Ali entourage and loose-end fight fans were drinking away what was left of the night in a city famous for its beer. Any one of them might have jumped me if they'd known I was temporary keeper of the world championship gloves.

After a minute, the door was opened by the most famous sportsman in the world. 'Ah, Norman the Doorman,' Muhammad Ali said, beckoning for me to follow him through the entrance hall into his luxury bedroom. Sitting up in a king-sized bed in her silk, off-the-shoulder negligee was the latest lady in his life. I took her to be Veronica Porche, who would soon become the third Mrs Ali.

'Baby, this is Norman the Doorman, a famous British sports press agent,' he said, awarding me an over-the-top introduction while studiously not mentioning the presumed

Veronica by name. Ali was notorious in boxing circles for his liking for female company, and it was none of my business who was in his bed. He was entitled to sleep with whom he liked.

Ali was wearing just a pair of cotton plaid pyjama briefs. Boxer shorts, I guess, which was appropriate. There were few signs on his handsome face or Michelangelo-chiselled body that he had just been involved in a fierce defence of his world title.

He walked to the huge fridge in the corner of the room and asked what I'd like to drink. At six o'clock in the morning a cup of tea would have gone down a treat. 'A Coke, please,' I said, suddenly shy in the big man's company, particularly as I felt in the way of him and his stunning companion.

'So what'd ya think of the fight?' he asked, pouring me a glass of Coke. I will repeat our conversation in full to give you an insight into the *real* Muhammad Ali, away from the roaring crowd.

'Richard did our country proud,' I replied honestly, 'though you beat him emphatically in the end. But he seemed to have you worried early on.'

'Certainly gave it his all and then some,' Ali said, sitting on the side of his bed and gesturing for me to take a seat in an armchair. 'Couldn't keep him on the canvas. Kept jumpin' up like a darn jack-in-the-box.'

Ali looked at me quizzically. 'Remind me when we first met, Stormin' Norman?' he said. 'Think it was in London.' Ali was calling me Stormin' Norman long before General Schwarzkopf laid claim to the moniker.

'May, 1963,' I said. 'You were training in an old gymnasium in Shepherd's Bush in west London back when you were known to the world as Cassius Clay. You were preparing for your first fight with Henry Cooper.'

'Ah, dear old Henry. Give him mah regards next time you see him. Very fond of that guy. Great human being, and he had the punch of a mule.'

'Also met you at Wembley Stadium when you sat at the back of the press box sleeping through the 1966 World Cup Final. You were in London for your title defence against Brian London at Earls Court.'

Ali chuckled.

'Took a lot of joshin' for goin' to sleep. Didn't mean to be disrespectful. I was on US time and couldn't keep mah eyes open. Soccer's never grabbed mah attention. Little boys and gals play it in the States. Didn't want to go to the match but Jack Solomons was desperate to publicise mah fight against Brian London. Guess it was one of England's greatest sportin' moments and I slept through it!'

'Did Richard ever have you in trouble tonight?' I asked.

'I'd say surprised rather than troubled. We'd been told he folded like a tent in the wind if anybody landed a hard punch. But he took plenty of mah best shots without goin' over.'

Ali paused, and briefly appeared puzzled. 'Yah had a good look at mah gloves, Norm?' he asked.

I pulled them out of the Puma holdall, two strawberry-red Everlast boxing gloves that had been bashing against Richard Dunn's head just over two hours earlier.

'Have a look inside,' Ali said.

Inside the right hand glove, written in biro, it said 'Ali won'. 'Now the left one,' instructed the Champ.

Written inside the left glove, 'WKO 5'.

'Wrote that in the dressing room before the fight,' he revealed in an almost matter-of-fact way. 'Helped pass the time and I like to give mahself challenges. Keeps yah on yah toes.'

'So you carried Richard for four rounds?' I asked, falteringly.

'Well I did have mah target of the fifth, but for those first four rounds he fought his heart out. Didn't shout about it before the fight, 'cos nothin' would have sold tickets. Had to buy up half the stadium to make sure people were watchin'. First time any boxer's paid for spectators to come and watch him fight! They'd hardly been anybody there if I hadn't paid for them GIs to have seats.'

He looked hard at me and shook his head slowly. 'Not much of a publicist, are yah Stormin' Norman.'

I was about to mount a defence about being there to sell tickets for ViewSport watchers at home when he added, 'Just kidding with yah, Norm. I knows yah were there workin' for Jarvis. He told me.'

ViewSport did make a profit on the fight. Meanwhile, I handed Ali the gloves and a permanent marker pen that I'd borrowed from hotel reception, and he signed each glove 'Muhammad Ali, 5.25.76'.

'Wish Chris Finnegan good luck from me,' he said. 'Met him and his brother several times in the UK. Terrible to have that eye damage. One of mah best friends Jimmy Ellis had to quit for the same reason. I help him as best I can by hirin' him as a sparrin' partner who I just dance with.'

Ali suddenly rolled over, leaning against his girlfriend as he laughed uncontrollably.

'Who was that mad guy yah sprung on me in the hotel corridor?' he asked, and then talking to his companion, 'This bad man only put a witch doctor on me. Told me I was d-o-o-m-e-d.'

'We brought him over to hypnotise Dunn,' I said, feeling embarrassed. 'Just a gimmick to try to sell tickets. He took it upon himself to try to hypnotise you.'

'Funniest thing yah've ever seen,' he said to his girlfriend. 'He was jumpin' up in front of me like a bullfrog, eyes out wide like Popeye.'

As I was about to leave with the precious gloves safely back in my holdall, Ali padded to a sideboard and took out a copy of his autobiography, *The Greatest*, and signed it to me, 'To Norman, best wishes Muhammad Ali ... May 25 76 ... Peace.'

That book still has pride of place on my bookshelf more than 47 years later. And the Ali-signed gloves were auctioned for £10,000 at Chris Finnegan's benefit night that weekend.

Ali then politely walked me to the door. 'See you around, Norman the Doorman,' he said, still laughing at the memory of Romark.

I waved at his lady, who gave me the sweetest of smiles.

I felt emotional, and managed to say, 'Look after yourself, Champ. Please get out of boxing soon. You're a legend.'

I could think of nobody else in the world (OK, perhaps Count Basie, Duke Ellington or Frank Sinatra) who could reduce me to a tongue-tied fool. It had been one of the most memorable chats of my life, and one day, I promised myself, I would record it in a book.

I was still feeling in an overwhelmed daze as I went in the express lift down to the lobby to await the return of the not-quite-conquering hero Richard Dunn. He was on his way back to the Hilton Hotel from the local hospital.

He had been punched almost senseless by the gloves that were in my bag.

You couldn't make it up.

Round Twelve

Confessions of a hypnotist

THE HOTEL lobby was still teeming with the flotsam and jetsam of the fight night, and I found a pack of my old press day pals monitoring the revolving doors at the main entrance. 'Richard's due back any moment,' *Daily Express* veteran Sydney Hulls told me. 'He went to hospital for a routine inspection. Hope they checked his brain. What a bashing he took.'

Within moments a Mercedes limousine pulled up and out got Richard in his Puma tracksuit, and accompanied by George Biddles and dear, loyal 'Pop' Devanney. The battered challenger wore dark glasses to mask his bruised and swollen eyes and he was clearly showing signs of utter exhaustion.

Then, something I never thought I'd see – there was a gathering of hard-bitten, cynical, world-travelled British sportswriters surrounding Richard Dunn and cheering and applauding him like fans at a pop concert.

Richard was both embarrassed and elated, and it was at that moment he realised that he had won an army of supporters for the astonishing bravery he had displayed against Ali. He was going home a hero. Beaten but not bowed.

No way was I going to show him the gloves on which Ali had scrawled his prediction, 'WKO 5'.

Suddenly a slender, pop-eyed man pushed his way through from the back of the press gang and threw his arms around a startled Dunn. It was a weeping, overwrought Romark.

'Richard, Richard,' he confessed through sobs, tears rolling down his contorted face, 'I turned your fists to iron but I forgot about your chin.'

Yep, couldn't make it up.

* * *

I went with Richard, George and Jimmy to their suite of rooms, where we were joined by a tearful Janet Dunn, George's wife Sarah, and a small group of the Dunn family and friends. As we enjoyed a good old cup of Yorkshire Tea, Richard was in the mood to talk about his great adventure. It was over now and he was starting to rerun it in his mind like a favourite film that suddenly became a horror movie:

'Well, I promised to give Ali t'fright of his life, and that's exactly what he got. I really clobbered him in those first two rounds. He were saying to me, "That all you got, sucker?" But I knew I were hurting him. I were hitting him as hard as I've hit anybody in my life.

'At one time in the second round he said, "Nice one, Dickie," after I'd caught him with a left hook. He were talking all t'time. Just like he did against Foreman. But he weren't gonna put me off.

'Mind you, even by his standards he went a bit far when I had him on the ropes, and he spotted that beautiful actress Candice Bergen looking up at us from the ringside. She were working for t'television company. What does Ali do while I'm trying to chin him? Winks at her!

'I kept chasing after him so hard that he changed tactics in t'third round and instead of dancing and jabbing decided to slug it out with me. It were like being on t'cobbles in Halifax. Biff, bang, wallop. We were both going for it, and I honestly thought I were going to get t'better of him.

'Then in t'fourth round he caught me a beauty of a right hand punch to the chin and I ran right into it. I thought, "Bloody 'ell's bells, better go down for a rest Dickie boy," and I took a count to give meself time to clear my head. It all seemed to be happening in slow motion.

'To be honest it's all a bit of a fog from there. I had this crazy idea if I could just connect once to his chin I could turn everything around, but he had me bouncing up and down like a bloody yo-yo. I were seeing two of the referee as he counted over me, so I knew I were in bother.

'George talked about pulling me out at end of t'fourth round but I told him no way. If I were going to lose, I were going down fighting. He'd been pointing towards where he were going to drop me, and that got me boiling mad. I went running after him and for a minute I honestly thought I were going to turn t'tables. Then he hit me! I found meself back on the canvas, think it were twice. Next I can remember the referee were holding me back from chasing after Ali again, and saying, "Enough, Herr Dunn. You cannot go on any longer."

'I were protesting about the stoppage, although I knew in my heart t'referee were doing me a favour. But I would have fought on, even though I didn't know where I were.

'My satisfaction is that I gave my all, like I said I would. No shame in getting beat by the greatest heavyweight who ever lived. I gave him a fright. He told me later that I'd given him a harder fight than any other Brit had given him, and that I could now be considered among the top contenders. I asked for a return fight, but he's not daft enough to agree to it. No matter what he might say, I hurt him tonight. I shook up The Greatest. Eeh, greatest night of my life.'

Richard was in a hyper mood and continuing to talk in rambling fashion as I left for my own room, still carrying the gloves that revealed in Muhammad Ali's own handwriting, 'WKO 5'.

* * *

On his return home to Bradford the next day, Richard got a rapturous reception as he was driven, with Janet, from the airport to the town hall in an open-topped white Rolls-Royce. Home is the hero, home from the war.

He was still holder of the British, Commonwealth and European titles and the drums were already beating for Richard to defend the crowns against an old nemesis, Joe Bugner, the fighter whose photograph adorned a lavatory seat at the Dunn gymnasium in Bradford.

It would not need Romark to motivate Richard Dunn (or Joe Bugner) for this one. They hated each other.

Round Thirteen

Showdown with Joe Bugner

THE FEISTY Richard Dunn and I were reunited five months later when he defended his three titles against former holder Joe Bugner, an opponent the Yorkshireman had always held in contempt. You could not help notice when visiting Dunn's old farm gymnasium in Underhill, Bradford, that for two years he had a lavatory seat pinned to the wall with a blown-up photograph of Bugner pasted inside. Hungarian-born Joe read about it and said, 'He will pay for that lack of respect.'

I was publicist for the Harry Levene-promoted fight at Wembley Arena in October 1976 and can smugly claim it was a sell-out show. They generated such genuine hatred against each other that the fight sold itself, something that Levene – the mean machine – was quick to point out when negotiating my fee.

With my strong Fleet Street links, I was able to place my ghosted life stories of both fighters in huge circulation Sunday newspapers, Dunn in the *Mirror* and Bugner in the *People*.

The remarkable thing about both stories is that each fighter claimed not to have known his father, and matchmaker Mickey Duff was only half joking when he said we should bill it as the 'Battle of the Bastards'.

Dunn had been demanding a showdown with Bugner for years, and had always dismissed him as the 'Sugar Plum Fairy'. He just did not rate a fighter he described as 'manufactured and only getting to the top because he has the right connections'.

Big Joe was six when he escaped with his mother from Hungary during the revolution against Russian occupation in 1956. He became a national English schoolboys discus champion when at school in Bedfordshire and developed a physique that had him likened to a Greek statue, and some – including Dunn – claimed he also moved like one.

He came under the wing of Anglo-Scot Andy Smith, a strong-willed puppeteer of his fighters. Critics doubted Joe's ability to take a punch after he was knocked out in the third round of his professional debut against the little-known Paul Brown. He was just 17. His opponent in his 15th fight, Ulric Regis, died following a savage fight with Bugner and it was believed from that day on the Hungarian never really had his heart in the Brutal Game.

Both Richard and Joe were coming off recent defeats by Muhammad Ali, Dunn with his brave but futile effort in Munich and Bugner following a 15-round dance in a 1975 world championship duel in the scorching heat of Kuala Lumpur.

Dunn watched the fight on television, and told anybody and everybody in hearing distance that Bugner should have been arrested for fraud. 'He cheated the public with that performance,' Richard fumed. 'Everyone should get their money back. He never made one attacking move. If I ever get to fight Ali, I'll win or finish up in hospital.'

He got his prediction half right in Munich, but every witness – including Ali – agreed that he had put up a better performance than Bugner, who went for an hour-long swim in his hotel pool after his strictly come dancing display against the champion.

Moving on to fight night at Wembley, and as Richard was making his way to the ring, picked out in a spotlight, a woman dashed out of the crowd and pushed a file of papers into his gloved hands. It turned out that she was his mother, and the papers were a writ suing him because she insisted he DID know who his father was (yes, still in the land of 'you couldn't make it up').

So Richard was not totally concentrating on the fight as the bell rang for round one. He was knocked down by the first hard punch, after just six seconds, never recovered and was flattened in two minutes 13 seconds of sheer mayhem. In that short, sensational time he was down twice before a right cross sent him crash-landing on to his back like an out-of-control parachutist for the full ten-second count. He was getting up as referee Harry Gibbs signalled a knockout and his outstretched arms hit Dunn, who fell over again in a total daze.

Those Ali punches had taken their toll and he had none of the punch resistance he had revealed so bravely in Munich.

Unbelievably, at 10am the next day a bruised and still confused Richard and I were in the lawyer's office at the *Mirror* in High Holborn trying to explain our story about him not knowing his father. Stop the fight, ref!

When it was pointed out to his mother that she would be charged all costs if the little matter of a DNA test went against her, the case was quietly dropped.

Dear old Richard went for one more pay day, a suicidal assignment against the fearsome-punching South African

Kallie Knoetze on his own turf in Johannesburg in September 1977. Predictably, he took the ten count in the fifth round.

He and Janet ploughed all their money into a hotel venture in Scarborough and when it ran into bankruptcy problems he returned to scaffolding for his daily bread. Working on an oil rig in the North Sea in 1989, he managed to break both legs in a 40ft fall. Doctors told him he would never walk again, but Richard being Richard was back on two feet again after 18 months as a hospital patient.

The sports-for-all stadium he had helped build in the 1970s was named the Richard Dunn Sports Centre in his honour, and when it was in danger of being demolished in 2019 the Historic England society came to the rescue by granting the building Grade II-listed status.

Like Richard, later sadly lost in a fog of dementia, it was considered a Yorkshire treasure. He has been lovingly looked after by his daughter Karen and son-in-law Greg Scott, a popular local TV presenter and voiceover artist. They put out a nationwide call for anybody to come up with video coverage of his 1976 European title triumph over Bernd August, and a Welsh film collector had recorded the three-round demolition of the German champion that earned Richard his tilt at Muhammad Ali.

'Richard's short-term memory is shot to pieces,' said Greg. 'But he can still get pleasure from things that happened many years ago and seeing his victory against August brought him huge joy.'

Anybody who witnessed his world championship challenge against Muhammad Ali – yes, simply The Greatest – will confirm that he was the bravest of British heroes.

Round Fourteen

The rise and fall of Romark

WHAT OF Romark? He kept bouncing into the headlines in a most bizarre way. His blindfolded driving stunt was eventually the subject of a case at Snaresbrook Crown Court, where he faced a charge of reckless driving. He was fined £100 and ordered to pay £220 costs. During the trial Romark revealed while being cross-examined that he could see perfectly through the blindfold because of two tiny, almost undetectable piercings in the fabric. This got him into trouble with the Magic Circle, where he had been a prominent member.

Circle president David Berglas was seething and said, 'Romark not only let down the rest of our profession but he let down the public, which enjoys being led to believe that a fairly simple trick is done by supernatural magic.'

Markham refused to apologise to the Circle, stating, 'It is immoral for magicians to pretend they are anything other than people who perform a good trick.'

As if Romark would have ever pretended!

A couple of years later I was working as a scriptwriter on a television show with comedian and entrepreneur Bob Monkhouse, and I told him about the Romark/Ali experience. I thought Bob was going to levitate. 'That bastard,' he said. 'Cheated me out of thousands of pounds. We were partners in a nightclub extravaganza in Newcastle in the late '60s and he emptied the bank account and disappeared to Africa. Conned me into bankrolling a project in which he was going to hypnotise people into stopping smoking and ran off with the money, leaving me with a mountain of debts. Made me want to start smoking!'

I looked deeper into Romark's background and discovered that he was a Geordie by birth and he had been in turn an auctioneer, actor and owner of an antiques showroom in Oxford before going into the ill-fated nightclub business with Monkhouse.

He then popped up in Durban in South Africa, billed in a one-man show as 'The World's Most Remarkable Brain'. One of his tricks was to hang himself on stage and then come back to life. Next he appeared in Hollywood projected as 'an extraordinary illusionist and hypnotist who will blow your mind'.

Back home to Britain and his native north-east, where he set out to hypnotise 1,000 people at Newcastle City Hall into stopping smoking. During the charade, six women collapsed and had to be revived by Markham himself after paramedics had failed. No plants, of course. Cynical, moi?

The BBC fell for his spiel when he assured them he could out-psych the young, spoon-bending Israeli Uri Geller, and he was given his own series, *The Man and His Mind*, which quickly died a death and was taken off air with viewers saying his illusions were an obvious fake.

He returned to his feud with Malcolm Allison in 1980. Halifax Town manager George Kirby wanted to wind Malcolm up before an FA Cup third round tie against Manchester City and he called Romark in to hypnotise his

Halifax players. They beat City 1-0 and Romark, of course, claimed the credit.

Markham then reinvented himself as a Harley Street hypnotherapist and was back in the headlines when he announced a hex on *The Sun* for trying to expose him as a fraud.

He was saving his most outrageous trick for last. Let me quote from *The Times* of 29 May 1982, under the capitalised headline 'TV HYPNOTIST JAILED FOR ROBBING MOTHER': 'It was claimed in court that Mr Ronald Markham, aka television hypnotist and illusionist Romark, had plundered his ailing mother's fortune with the aim of setting up a new home in Hollywood.

'Markham, aged 55, had denied 14 charges of theft and fraud, and his wife pleaded not guilty to being party to them. It was claimed that while Markham's mother, 79-year-old Emma Goldman, was gravely ill, her son and his new wife, Ursula, had taken £68,000's worth of her silver, antiques and jewellery. Mr Markham had forged letters and his mother's signature to withdraw over £47,000 from her savings account.

'Following a guilty verdict, the judge sentenced Mr Markham to 18 months' imprisonment and his wife to nine.'

I have to say yet again, you couldn't make it up.

Romark was released early from prison on health grounds, and died following another stroke in Torbay, Devon, in December 1982. He was 56.

Mickey Duff said, 'He always gave me bad vibes and I never fell for all his bullshit. As I told him to his two faces, he was a charlatan.'

I always wondered about Mickey's undisguised contempt for Romark when we were in Munich, and he told me, 'Jarvis knew all about his history and had tipped me off that he was a con artist. Robbing his own old sick mother. How low can a snake go?'

Malcolm Allison, then managing Sporting Lisbon in Portugal after getting sacked by Manchester City following the defeat by Halifax, said simply, 'Good riddance.'

Somehow, I can still feel I have fists of iron.

Romark. Ronald Markham. Definitely one of my most unforgettable characters.

Round Fifteen

A tribute to Muhammad Ali

SO WE arrive at the final round of a book that is different to any other I have written in my 65-year career scribbling words for a living, acting as hidden observer of champions and clowns performing at the very top of the sports mountain. This is the 120th book I have had published, and never before have I said so many times, 'You couldn't make it up.'

From Romark trying to drive blindfolded across London and his attempted hypnosis of the greatest fighter who ever lived, Richard Dunn being served with a writ by his own mother on the way to the ring, interviewing Muhammad Ali in his bedroom two hours after his championship defence – it has been tales of the unexpected all the way to the final bell.

But, sadly, I have to finish our journey on a downbeat note. Yes, it's an anthem of acclaim to the greatest – unquestionably The Greatest – heavyweight fighter who ever climbed into the roped square, and a salute to the bravery of the Lion of Yorkshire, Richard Dunn.

Yet the more I researched, probed, explored and analysed Ali's fights the more I became distraught and depressed by the painful and pitiful destinies of not only Ali himself but of the now lost-to-dementia Dunn and so many of Ali's opponents.

It helped to magnify the love–hate relationship I have with boxing. I love the theatre, the drama, the skill, the bravery, the naked violence of the sport. I hate what it does to the health of its combatants, the winners as well as the losers. It weighs heavily on my conscience, yet I keep returning to the ringside like an eyewitness going back to the scene of the car crash in the hope of seeing another one.

You need to be in and around the fight game to understand that there is an acceptance of what is almost a beauty in the brutality of the sport, but we who do the observing from the safe side of the ropes do not have to carry beyond the stadium the consequence of the punishment caused by the punches. We go home with thrilling memories, while the pugilists take home the cuts, bruises and the pain.

The evidence is here in the previous pages that Ali and the beyond brave Dunn – and virtually all Ali's opponents – suffered life-harming damage to their health so that promoters, managers, trainers, TV and broadcasters, reporters and fight fans – yes, and publicists – could feed off their industry, their skill and their courage.

Many of those fighters who got to share the ring with Ali – Dunn, modestly – earned money beyond the dreams of avarice in return for their gladiatorial skills, but what use is wealth when later in life they become lost in a desert of dementia, with no memory of their achievements and, in most cases, parted from their hard-earned cash?

Ali outlived 32 of his 54 opponents, most of them dying from causes linked to the effects of taking punches in the ring. Of those still living, more than a dozen are suffering from pugilistic dementia, or to be painfully blunt, punch-drunkenness.

After being diagnosed with Parkinson's disease in 1984, there was a gradual decline in Ali's health. But, with the staunch support of his fourth wife Lonnie, the heavily medicated former champion handled his debilitating illness with dignity and courage, and never felt sorry for himself or offered a critical word against the raw violence of boxing before his passing in Arizona on 3 June 2016 at the age of 74.

Nobody who saw that hugely emotional moment when he lit the flame to open the 1996 Atlanta Olympics will forget his spirit, his pride and his grandeur as he defied the challenge of Parkinson's to carry out his duty. Muhammad Ali lit up the world.

I was privileged to be in Ali's company several times following his illness, and on each occasion he stressed that he was not looking for pity and accepted his condition as a challenge. He continued to worship Allah and insisted he had no regrets about a boxing career that sensible judges consider went several fights too far.

Those of us who saw him dig deep to defeat the courageous Dunn and cared about him were desperate for him to hang up his gloves, but his enlarged ego forced him to go to the well far too many times.

He battled through seven more contests after the defence against Richard Dunn, not including his farcical 15-round draw in a box-wrestling gimmick match against Japanese giant Antonio Inoki. Ali's fee for lost dignity was a mere $6m.

He had wars with Ken Norton, Earnie Shavers, Leon Spinks (two 15-round battles) and those who put him into the ring with Larry Holmes should have been locked up. His former sparring partner stopped him for the only inside-the-distance defeat of his 65-fight career. I was not alone in crying as I watched him having to reluctantly surrender at the end of ten brutal rounds.

There is a generation growing up who never had the privilege of seeing Ali in action in the ring. They only know him as famous for being famous, and their image of him is of a shuffling wreck of a man who coped as best he could with the ravages of Parkinson's, the one deadly opponent he could not beat. Those who claimed it was not caused by boxing are lying to themselves.

Youngsters should know that at his peak Ali was one of the most beautifully and perfectly sculptured boxing champions of them all, and – as he kept reminding us – he was not only The Greatest but also The Prettiest. It was always said with tongue in cheek, but you could not deny the truth of his boasts.

Few from the Ali camp are left. Angelo Dundee, Bundini Brown, Ferdie Pacheco, Jimmy Ellis, Herbert Muhammad, commentator Howard Cosell, masseur Luis Sarriar and personal photographer Howard Bingham are all gone now to the great boxing ring in the sky. Those of us who are still here (just) have a duty to tell people how exceptional Muhammad Ali was both as a boxer and as a man.

It is an important part of his legend that he first came to prominence in an unfair and unjust world in which too many were judged by the colour of their skin rather than their abilities. He had to overcome huge prejudices in an era when black athletes could be the best in their sport, yet not sit in the front of the bus in some parts of the United States.

Ali – who daringly dropped what he called his slave name of Cassius Clay – transcended his sport to become arguably the most famous person in the world. He not only got to the front of the bus, he drove it. But the bitterness of those early days when he could not be served in a whites-only restaurant or drink from certain water fountains never left him.

I vividly recall a quiet, casual conversation we had in Munich away from the madding crowd. Ali was as relaxed as I had ever known him, and was popping questions at me about my life and how I'd got into the boxing PR business. For a man who hogged the spotlight when in publicity-seeking mode, he was gracious and respectful in private conversation, and keen to learn and digest anything new. I am a witness to the fact that he was a good listener as well as the braggart he presented to the public.

'Yah're like me, y'know,' he said. 'Yah have to tell lies to get bums on to seats. I have to pretend to hate mah opponents, yet there are very few that I have not liked and I always respect their bravery for getting into that loneliest of places, the boxing ring. I sometimes feel I went too far with mah insults of Smokin' Joe but, heck, somebody had to get them tickets sold.'

'You must mean some of the nasty things you say about them,' I offered. 'Look at the way you belittled Henry Cooper by calling him a crippled old bum.'

'Listen, when I get into that ring against anybody I'm secretly as scared as hell,' he confided, almost in a whisper. 'Just take Henry, for example. He had a left hook that could send an astronaut to the Moon without a rocket. But I had to make him think he was no worry to me at all. So I used the insults as a weapon, demoralising my opponents to make them feel small and inferior. I'm frightened when I get into the ring. I want the man in the other corner to feel even more scared. Fear is a factor few outside our sport understand. If yah can conquer fear, yah have the biggest obstacle out of the way. But if yah've got a George Foreman, a Smokin' Joe or a Ken Norton coming at yah, man, believe me, only a fool would not be scared. And I ain't no fool.'

Islam remained the most vital presence in Ali's life right to the end of his time, a driving force that became an obsession. He never pushed his views on you in private, but once you were talking to him on the record with a microphone and notebook in sight, he would become a preacher of Islamic ideas and ideals.

White extremists hated Ali for his controversial views, but we're all shaped by experiences and environment and Ali was black, proud and said it out loud at a time when the Civil Rights Movement in the United States was going full blast. Ali's opinions split the nation, particularly after his refusal to join the US Army because he had 'no quarrel with them Vietcong. They ain't never called me a nigger.'

Soon, most fair-minded people were echoing Ali's view against the obscene war in Vietnam. He was brave enough to put his career on the line for peace. What a man.

Muhammad Ali had flaws, and many of his pronouncements were poisoned with bigotry and racism. But as a pugilist and a publicist, an entertainer and symbol of defiance in and out of the ring there has been nobody to touch him.

For me, Muhammad Ali will always be The Greatest.

And I know that a certain Richard Dunn agrees with that assessment. 'Greatest sportsman and showman who ever lived,' he told me long before dementia descended like a black cloud on his memory. 'I were chuffed to share the ring with him and loved every minute of it.'

You couldn't make it up.

The Muhammad Ali Timeline

This is an updated version of the fact file that I prepared for the British press contingent in Munich to report the Ali–Dunn world title fight:

Born: 17 January 1942

Birthplace: Louisville, Kentucky

Original name: Cassius Marcellus Clay, Jr, named after his father Cassius (Cash) Clay, a shop sign and billboard painter, who was himself given his name in honour of the white 19th-century abolitionist and politician of the same name.

Mother: Odessa (Grady) Clay, who was a household domestic.

Early religion: Cassius Sr was a Methodist, but allowed Odessa to bring up both Cassius and his younger brother Rudolph 'Rudy' Clay (later Rahman Ali) in her faith as a Baptist.

Ancestry: He is a descendant of pre-Civil War era slaves in the American South, and is predominantly of African-American descent, with Irish, English, and Italian ancestry.

Marriages: Sonji Roi (August 1964–January 1966, divorced), Kalilah Tolona (Belinda Boyd) (August 1967–January 1977, divorced), Veronica Porche (June 1977–January 1986, divorced), Yolanda (Lonnie) Williams (19 November 1986).

Children: with Kalilah – Maryum (1968), Rasheeda and Jamilla (1970), Muhammad Ibo (1972); with Patricia Harvell – Miya (1971); with Aaisha Fletcher – Khalilah (1974); with Veronica – Hana (1976) and Laila (1977); adopted with Yolanda – Assad (1986).

1954: Starts boxing after reporting the theft of his bicycle to a policeman called Joe Martin, who persuades him to take his anger out in the gymnasium that he runs in Louisville. In a six-year amateur career, Clay wins 100 of 108 contests, including six Kentucky Golden Gloves championships.

1959: Wins the first of two National Golden Gloves titles as a light-heavyweight and qualifies for the US Olympic team. Graduates from Louisville Central High School.

1960: Wins Olympic gold medal in Rome, clearly outpointing Poland's Zbigniew Pietrzykowski in the final. Turns professional on his return home, signing with a syndicate of Kentucky businessmen. Outpoints Tunney Hunsaker over eight rounds in his professional debut in Louisville on 29 October. Refuses to be trained by Archie Moore and joins the Miami camp of Angelo Dundee.

1963: Dropped by a left hook from Henry Cooper in the fourth round of his 19th fight at Wembley Stadium. The bell comes to his rescue, and he wins on a cut eye stoppage in the fifth round, as he predicted.

1964, 25 February: Sonny Liston quits on his stool at the end of six rounds and Clay becomes world heavyweight champion. He is 22 and in the 20th fight of his professional career. He roars, 'I done shook up the world.'

Later announces that he has joined the Nation of Islam and that in future he will answer only to the name of Muhammad Ali.

1965: Wins rematch with Liston on a controversial first-round knockout. His first fight as Muhammad Ali. Knocks Liston out with what becomes known as 'the phantom punch'.

1966: Splits with the Louisville Sponsoring Group and his new manager is Herbert Muhammad, a son of Nation of Islam leader, Elijah.

1967: Refuses induction into the US Army as a conscientious objector, saying, 'Man, I ain't got no quarrel with them Vietcong. No Vietcong ever called me nigger.'

The World Boxing Association strips him of his world title. New York and other states revoke his licence to box. Convicted in federal court of violating Selective Service laws, sentenced to five years in prison, and fined $10,000. He is freed on bail pending an appeal, and the jail sentence is later quashed.

1967–70: Forced out of boxing, he makes a living giving anti-war lectures at colleges and appears on Broadway in the short-lived musical *Buck White*.

1970, 26 October: Stops Jerry Quarry in three rounds in his first professional fight in more than three years.

1971, 8 March: His first defeat, outpointed by Joe Frazier in the 'fight of the century' at Madison Square Garden, New York. Ali and Frazier split a $5m purse.

1971, 28 June: The US Supreme Court reverses Ali's Selective Service violation conviction in a unanimous ruling.

1972, 20 September: Stops Floyd Patterson in seven rounds, retaining the NABF title.

1973, 31 March: Suffers broken jaw when losing the NABF title to Ken Norton on points over 12 rounds.

1973, 10 September: Regains the NABF title with a 12-round points revenge win over Norton.

1974, 28 January: Outpoints Joe Frazier over 12 rounds to retain his NABF title. Both Ali and Frazier fined $5,000 for brawling in a TV studio before the fight.

1974, 30 October: The 'Rumble in the Jungle' in Kinshasa, Zaire (now Democratic Republic of the Congo). Ali uses 'rope-a-dope' tactics to take the world heavyweight title from George Foreman with a sensational eighth-round knockout victory.

1975: Quits the Nation of Islam to practise the more traditional Islamic faith. 1 October: Wins the 'Thrilla in Manila' against Joe Frazier, who is retired by his corner at the end of 14 brutal rounds.

1978, 15 February: Loses his heavyweight title to Leon Spinks on a split decision over 15 rounds.

1978, 15 September: Becomes world heavyweight champion for a record third time when regaining the title from Spinks with a unanimous 15-round points decision.

1979, 26 June: Announces his retirement from professional boxing.

1980, 2 October: Comes out of retirement for a guaranteed purse of $8m, and is retired after ten punishing rounds in his challenge for the title held by his former sparring partner, Larry Holmes. He is now showing the first signs of Parkinson's disease.

1981, 11 December: Loses on points over ten rounds to Trevor Berbick in the Bahamas. It is his last fight.

1984: Reveals that he has Parkinson's disease, a disorder of the central nervous system.

1990, 27 November: Meets with Saddam Hussein in Baghdad, in an attempt to negotiate the release of Americans held hostage in Iraq and Kuwait, and comes home the following week with 14 hostages.

1996, 19 July: Lights the torch at the opening ceremony to the Olympic Games in Atlanta. The world is shocked to see how badly he is affected by Parkinson's.

2000, 23 October: Appointed United Nations Messenger of Peace.

2005, 9 November: Presented with the Presidential Medal of Freedom by President George W. Bush.

2005, 21 November: The Muhammad Ali Center opens in Louisville, Kentucky.

2006, 11 April: Entertainment and licensing firm CKX announces that it is paying Ali $50m in exchange for 80 per cent of whatever it makes selling his name and likeness. It forms a company called G.O.A.T., which stands for 'Greatest of All Time'.

2013, October: Despite scare stories that he is 'at death's door', Ali attends a Three Days of Greatness celebration at the Muhammad Ali Center in his hometown of Louisville, Kentucky, where Muhammad Ali Humanitarian Awards are handed out.

2016, 3 June: Muhammad Ali dies in hospital in Scottsdale, Arizona, at the age of 74.

His funeral on 10 June stops his hometown of Louisville, Kentucky. Ex-president Bill Clinton delivers one of many eulogies. Mike Tyson and actor Will Smith, who portrayed him in the biopic *The Greatest*, are among the pallbearers.

He sure shook up the world.

Muhammad Ali Ring Record

1960

Oct 29	Tunny Hunsaker	Louisville	Wpts6
Dec 27	Herbert Siler	Miami	Wrsf4

1961

Jan 17	Anthony Esperti	Miami	Wrsf3
Feb 7	Jim Robinson	Miami	Wrsf1
Feb 21	Donnie Fleeman	Miami	Wrsf7
April 19	Lamar Clark	Louisville	Wko2
June 26	Duke Sabedong	Las Vegas	Wpts10
July 22	Alonzo Johnson	Louisville	Wpts10
Oct 7	Alex Miteff	Louisville	Wrsf6
Nov 29	Willi Besmanoff	Louisville	Wrsf7

1962

Feb 10	Sonny Banks	New York City	Wrsf4
Feb 28	Don Warner	Miami	Wrsf4
Apr 23	George Logan	Los Angeles	Wrsf4
May 19	Billy Daniels	New York City	Wrsf7
July 20	Alejandro Lavorante	Los Angeles	Wko5
Nov 15	Archie Moore	Los Angeles	Wrsf4

1963

Jan 24	Charlie Powell	Pittsburgh	Wko3
Mar 13	Doug Jones	New York City	Wpts10
Jun 18	Henry Cooper	Wembley	Wrsf5

1964

| Feb 25 | Sonny Liston | Miami | Wret6 |

(won world heavyweight title; changed named to Muhammad Ali)

1965

| May 25 | Sonny Liston | Maine | Wko1 |
| Nov 22 | Floyd Patterson | Las Vegas | Wrsf12 |

1966

Mar 29	George Chuvalo	Toronto	Wpts15
May 21	Henry Cooper	Highbury	Wrsf6
Aug 6	Brian London	Earls Court	Wko3
Sep 10	Karl Mildenberger	Frankfurt	Wrsf12
Nov 14	Cleveland Williams	Houston	Wrsf3

1967

| Feb 6 | Ernie Terrell | Houston | Wpts15 |
| Mar 22 | Zora Folley | New York City | Wko7 |

1970

| Oct 26 | Jerry Quarry | Atlanta | Wrsf3 |
| Dec 7 | Oscar Bonavena | New York City | Wrsf15 |

1971

Mar 8	Joe Frazier	New York City	Lpts15
Jul 26	Jimmy Ellis	Houston	Wrsf12
Nov 17	Buster Mathis	Houston	Wpts12
Dec 26	Jürgen Blin	Zürich	Wko7

1972

Apr 1	Mac Foster	Tokyo	Wpts15
May 1	George Chuvalo	Vancouver	Wpts12
Jun 27	Jerry Quarry	Las Vegas	Wrsf7
Jul 19	Alvin Lewis	Dublin	Wrsf11
Sep 20	Floyd Patterson	New York City	Wrsf7
Nov 21	Bob Foster	Nevada	Wko8

1973

Feb 14	Joe Bugner	Las Vegas	Wpts12
Mar 31	Ken Norton	San Diego	Lpts12
Sep 10	Ken Norton	Inglewood	Wpts12
Oct 20	Rudi Lubbers	Jakarta	Wpts12

1974

Jan 28	Joe Frazier	New York City	Wpts12
Oct 30	George Foreman	Kinshasa	Wko8

(regained world heavyweight title)

1975

Mar 24	Chuck Wepner	Cleveland	Wrsf15
May 16	Ron Lyle	Las Vegas	Wrsf11
Jun 30	Joe Bugner	Kuala Lumpur	Wpts15
Oct 1	Joe Frazier	Manila	Wret14

1976

Feb 20	Jean-Pierre Coopman	San Juan	Wko5
Apr 30	Jimmy Young	Landover, MD	Wpts15
May 24	Richard Dunn	Munich	Wrsf5
Sep 28	Ken Norton	New York City	Wpts15

1977

May 16	Alfredo Evangelista	Landover, MD	Wpts15
Sep 29	Earnie Shavers	New York City	Wpts15

1978

Feb 15	Leon Spinks	Las Vegas	Lpts15
Sep 15	Leon Spinks	New Orleans	Wpts15

(won world heavyweight title for record third time)

1980

Oct 2	Larry Holmes	Las Vegas	Lret10
Dec 11	Trevor Berbick	Nassau	Lpts10

The Things Ali Said

A collection of Muhammad Ali quotes that I helped put together with my friends at the BBC on the day of his passing on 3 June 2016:

'To make America the greatest is my goal, so I beat the Russian and I beat the Pole. And for the USA won the medal of gold. The Greeks said you're better than the Cassius of old.' *After winning Olympic light-heavyweight gold medal at the 1960 Games in Rome.*

'Hey Floyd – I seen you fight! Someday I'm gonna whup you! Don't you forget, I am The Greatest!' *To the then world heavyweight champion Floyd Patterson during the 1960 Olympic Games.*

'Archie's been living off the fat of the land; I'm here to give him his pension plan. Moore will fall in four [he did].' *Before fighting Ol' Archie Moore.*

'Sonny Liston is nothing. The man can't talk. The man can't fight. The man needs talking lessons. The man needs boxing lessons. And since he's gonna fight me, he needs falling lessons.' *Before fighting world heavyweight champion Sonny Liston in February 1964.*

That's the volcanic and voluble matchmaker Mickey Duff in the centre as Dunn and Ali promote the world heavyweight title fight that few people wanted to pay to see.

Richard enjoys being frisked at Heathrow on his way to his title challenge against Muhammad Ali. He had nothing to declare on the homeward journey, other than he had done his best.

Trainer Jimmy 'Pops' Devanney looks on from his motorbike as Richard gives his brother-in-law Lawrence a piggy back during a training run in Munich the week before the fight with Ali.

Romark, real name Roland Markham. The Man Who Put a Curse on Muhammad Ali. He was eccentric to the point that Richard Dunn described him as 'barmy'. Here he is driving the conventional way, without a blindfold!

Muhammad Ali, The Greatest and The Prettiest, takes a breather while training for his title defence against British bulldog Richard Dunn.

Richard Dunn in traditional boxing pose. He was ready to give Muhammad Ali the fight and fright of his life but without the influence of hypnotist Romark.

It's the fourth round, and Ali cuts loose after a promising start by Richard the Lionheart, who suddenly finds himself on the way to the canvas for the first of six counts.

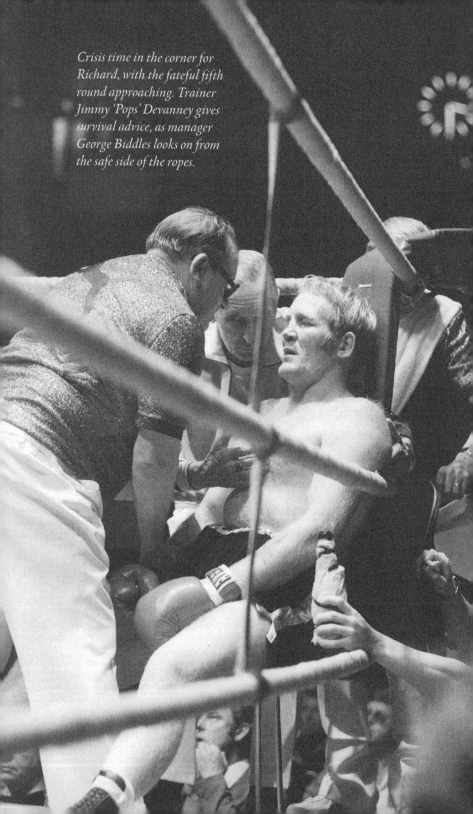

Crisis time in the corner for Richard, with the fateful fifth round approaching. Trainer Jimmy 'Pops' Devanney gives survival advice, as manager George Biddles looks on from the safe side of the ropes.

The end is nigh for the Bradford Bull as he goes down for the last time in the fifth round. German referee Herbert Tomser stopped it when he bravely got up yet again.

Bradford gave Richard a hero's welcome home the day after his title challenge against Muhammad Ali. 'Imagine what the turnout would have been if I'd won,' said a proud but rueful Dunn.

Richard Dunn signals at the weigh-in that the triple title fight with Joe Bugner will be over in two rounds. He was one round out … knocked cold in the first by the Hungarian-born heavyweight. That's promoter Harry Levene and Bugner's Svengali manager Andy Smith in the centre.

'Why, Chump, I bet you scare yourself to death just starin' in the mirror. You ugly bear! You ain't never fought nobody but tramps and has-beens. You call yourself a world champion? You're too old and slow to be champion!' *To Sonny Liston in the build-up to their first fight.*

'I'll hit Liston with so many punches from so many angles he'll think he's surrounded.' *Also in the build-up to facing Liston.*

'I shook up the world! I done shook up the world!' *After beating Liston in 1964.*

'I'll beat him so bad, he'll need a shoehorn to put his hat on.' *Before beating Floyd Patterson in 1965.*

'You have to give him credit – he put up a good fight for one and a half rounds.' *After knocking out Britain's Brian London in three rounds.*

'What's my name, fool? What's my name?' *To Ernie Terrell during their 1967 fight – Terrell had refused to call him Muhammad Ali.*

'I hit Bonavena so hard it jarred his kinfolks all the way back in Argentina.' *After beating Oscar Bonavena in December 1970.*

'I'm gonna do to Buster what the Indians did to Custer.' *Before beating Buster Mathis in November 1971.*

'I never thought of losing, but now that it's happened, the only thing is to do it right. That's my obligation to all the people who believe in me. We all have to take defeats in life.' *After losing to Ken Norton in 1973.*

'You say I'm not the man I was ten years ago. Well, I talked to your wife and she says you're not the man you were ten years ago!' *Ali to legendary boxing commentator Howard Cosell.*

'I've seen George Foreman shadow boxing and the shadow won.' *Before knocking out Foreman in their classic 'Rumble in the Jungle' clash in 1974.*

'I done wrestled with an alligator, I done tussled with a whale; handcuffed lightning, thrown thunder in jail; only last week, I murdered a rock, injured a stone, hospitalised a brick; I'm so mean I make medicine sick.' *Before the 'Rumble in the Jungle'.*

'That all you got, George?' *During the 'Rumble in the Jungle'.*

'The fight is won or lost far away from witnesses – behind the lines, in the gym, and out there on the road, long before I dance under those lights.' *On his training routine.*

On his three duels with Smokin' Joe Frazier:

'Joe Frazier is so ugly that when he cries, the tears turn around and go down the back of his head.'

'Frazier is so ugly he should donate his face to the US Bureau of Wildlife.'

'Any black person who's for Joe Frazier is a traitor. The only people rooting for Joe Frazier are white people in suits, Alabama sheriffs and members of the Ku Klux Klan. I'm fighting for the little man in the ghetto.'

'It will be a killer and a chiller and a thriller when I get the gorilla in Manila.' *Before the 'Thrilla in Manila' in 1975.*

'I always bring out the best in men I fight, but Joe Frazier, I'll tell the world right now, brings out the best in me. I'm gonna tell ya, that's one helluva man, and God bless him.' *After the 'Thrilla in Manila', which Ali won.*

'I said a lot of things in the heat of the moment that I shouldn't have said. Called him names I shouldn't have called him. I apologise for that. I'm sorry. It was all meant to promote the fight.' *In a moment of contrition after the 'Thrilla in Manila' against Joe Frazier.*

Ali on politics and personalities:

'Boxing is a lot of white men watching two black men beat each other up. Cassius Clay is a slave name. I didn't choose it, and I didn't want it. I am Muhammad Ali, a free name, and I insist people use it when speaking to me and of me.'

'Nobody has to tell me that this is a serious business. I'm not fighting one man. I'm fighting a lot of men, showing a lot of 'em, here is one man they couldn't defeat, couldn't conquer. My mission is to bring freedom to 30 million black people.' *Before Ali's fight against Jerry Quarry in 1970.*

'I am America. I am the part you won't recognise, but get used to me. Black, confident, cocky. My name, not yours. My religion, not yours. My goals, my own. Get used to me.'

'We were brought here 400 years ago for a job. Why don't we get out and build our own nation and quit begging for jobs? We'll never be free until we own our own land. We're 40 million people and we don't have two acres that's truly ours.'

'I'm gonna fight for the prestige, not for me, but to uplift my little brothers who are sleeping on concrete floors today in America. Black people who are living on welfare, black people who can't eat, black people who don't know no knowledge of themselves, black people who don't have no future.'

'I know I got it made while the masses of black people are catchin' hell, but as long as they ain't free, I ain't free.'

'What's really hurting me – the name Islam is involved, and Muslim is involved and causing trouble and starting hate and violence. Islam is not a killer religion, Islam means peace. I couldn't just sit home and watch people label Muslims as the reason for this problem.' *In the aftermath of the 2001 World Trade Center attacks.*

On refusing to serve in the United States Army:

'Why should they ask me to put on a uniform and go 10,000 miles from home and drop bombs and bullets on brown people in Vietnam while so-called Negro people in Louisville are treated like dogs and denied simple human rights?'

'Man, I ain't got no quarrel with them Vietcong. No Vietcong ever called me nigger.'

'I'm not going 10,000 miles from home to help murder and burn another poor nation simply to continue the domination of white slave masters of the darker people the world over.'

His sayings:

'Float like a butterfly, sting like a bee, his hands can't hit what his eyes can't see.'

'I am The Greatest!'

'I'm not The Greatest, I'm the Double Greatest. Not only do I knock 'em out, I pick the round. I'm the boldest, the prettiest, the most superior, most scientific, most skilfullest fighter in the ring today.'

'People don't realise what they had until it's gone. Like President Kennedy, nobody like him. Like the Beatles, there will never be anything like them. Like my man, Elvis Presley. I was the Elvis of boxing.'

'I don't want to fight to be an old man … I'm gonna only fight five or six years, make me two or three million dollars and quit fighting.'

'It's hard to be humble when you're as great as I am.'

'The fact is, I was never too bright in school. I ain't ashamed of it, though. I mean, how much do school principals make a month? I said I was "The Greatest", I never said I was the smartest!'

'At home I am a nice guy – but I don't want the world to know. Humble people, I've found, don't get very far.'

'When you can whup any man in the world, you never know peace. There's always someone thinks he's a faster gun. Then they get in the ring with me and, too late, they find out they was wrong. Damn!'

'Champions aren't made in gyms, champions are made from something they have deep inside them – a desire, a dream, a vision. They have to have last-minute stamina, they have to be a little faster, they have to have the skill and the will. But the will must be stronger than the skill.'

'A man who views the world the same at 50 as he did at 20 has wasted 30 years of his life.'

'If you even dream of beating me, you better wake up and apologise.'

'I love to see my name where everyone can read it. Someday I'm gonna see it in bright, bright lights.'

'I won't miss fighting – fighting will miss me.'

'I'm so fast that last night I turned off the light switch in my hotel room and was in bed before the room was dark.'

'Maybe my Parkinson's is God's way of reminding me what is important. It slowed me down and caused me to listen rather than talk. Actually, people pay more attention to me now because I don't talk as much.'

'I always liked to chase the girls. Parkinson's stops all that. Now I might have a chance to go to Heaven.'

'Will they ever have another fighter who writes poems, predicts rounds, beats everybody, makes people laugh, makes people cry and is as tall and extra pretty as me?'

You couldn't make him up.

PART TWO

A History of the Heavyweights

As a bonus to the main story of the Muhammad Ali v Richard Dunn title fight, we present a history of the heavyweights from John L. Sullivan to Tyson Fury. It's a complete breakdown of all world heavyweight champions for the past 100-plus years.

Compiled by Norman and Michael Giller

JOHN. L. SULLIVAN 1882–1892
Born: Roxbury, Mass., 15 October 1858
Died: Abington, Mass., 2 February 1918
Height: 5ft 10in
Weight: 13st 6lb (188lb)
Reach: 74in
Chest: 43–48in
Fist: 14in
Nickname: The Boston Strong Boy
Career span: 1878–1905
Record: 42 fights, 38 wins (33 KOs*), three draws, one loss
Age at which title was won: 26 (35th fight)
*Including stoppages as well as count-outs

THERE was no greater hero in American sport than John Lawrence Sullivan, the last of the bare-knuckle champions. He was a larger-than-life character who earned his 'Boston Strong Boy' nickname by displaying astonishing feats of strength. When he was just 16 he lifted a streetcar back on its rails, and he could hoist a full barrel of beer above his head like a weightlifter. Mind you, he usually first preferred to drink the barrel dry. Modesty never became him and he used to swagger into bar rooms and shout, 'I'll fight any man in the house.' There were never any takers!

A self-confessed womaniser, he had an enormous capacity for drink until in his later years when he travelled the United States as an evangelist preaching against the evils of alcohol.

He won the bare-knuckle version of the world heavyweight title in 1882 when he battered Tipperary's Paddy Ryan into submission in nine rounds in Mississippi City. When they met in a return wearing gloves in New York City three years later, police clambered into the ring and stopped the fight in the first round to save Ryan from annihilation.

Sullivan was crowned Queensberry world heavyweight champion when he beat Dominick McCaffrey over six rounds in Cincinnati on 29 August 1885. His most famous victory came when he knocked out Irishman Jake Kilrain in the 75th round of a brutal battle to retain his bare-knuckle title in 1889. It was the last fight staged under London Prize Ring Rules.

Although Sullivan was generally considered to have been world heavyweight champion, there is a school of thought among boxing historians that he should be regarded as a U.S. champion only. His one international match of consequence was against the English pugilist Charley Mitchell at Chantilly on 10 March 1888. An exhausting battle ended in a draw after 39 rounds.

Adding to the reluctance of some experts to accept him as a world champion is that Sullivan declined to fight the exceptional Australian black heavyweight Peter Jackson, leaning on the controversial colour line. But as far as American fight fans were concerned, Sullivan came into the 'national treasure' category.

Grown men cried when a potbellied, out-of-condition Sullivan was knocked out by James J. Corbett in the 21st round in New Orleans on 7 September 1892. Both men wore 5oz boxing gloves. It was Sullivan's only defeat in 42 fights. He retired after a couple of exhibition bouts, toured as an actor, was a preacher and remained an idol until his death at the age of 59.

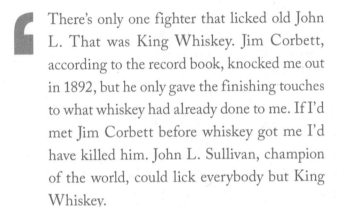 There's only one fighter that licked old John L. That was King Whiskey. Jim Corbett, according to the record book, knocked me out in 1892, but he only gave the finishing touches to what whiskey had already done to me. If I'd met Jim Corbett before whiskey got me I'd have killed him. John L. Sullivan, champion of the world, could lick everybody but King Whiskey.

JAMES J. CORBETT 1892–1897

Born: San Francisco, 1 September 1866
Died: Bayside, Long Island, 18 February 1933
Height: 6ft 1in
Weight: 13st (182lb)
Reach: 73in
Chest: 38–42in
Fist: 12.75in
Nickname: Gentleman Jim
Career span: 1884–1903
Record: 19 fights, 11 wins (seven KOs), two draws, four losses (three by KO), two no contest
Age at which title was won: 26 (13th fight)

JAMES J. Corbett was one of the pioneers of scientific boxing who believed that the sport should be as much about avoiding punches as landing them. He was never a devastating puncher, but a master tactician who nullified the work of his opponents by clever footwork and smart defensive strategy. It was a long time before the American public warmed to this former bank clerk after he had beaten their hero for all seasons, John L. Sullivan, who was used to fighting toe-to-toe sluggers and was outboxed by the elusive and fitter challenger.

Like Sullivan, Corbett was the son of an Irishman but he was the complete opposite to the Bostonian braggart both with his style inside the ring and his behaviour outside. He was a dandy dresser, articulate and quietly spoken. His good manners earned him the nickname 'Gentleman Jim', which was the title of the biographical film in which Errol Flynn portrayed Corbett.

He earned a crack at the title by fighting a draw over 61 rounds with Peter Jackson, the black West Indian who Sullivan had refused to fight 'on grounds of colour'.

In his first defence of the title, Corbett knocked out Englishman Charlie Mitchell in three rounds at Jacksonville on 25 January 1894. This was the one and only time Corbett lost his temper in the ring. Mitchell hurled a volley of verbal abuse at him as the referee was giving his final centre-of-the-ring instructions.

Mitchell had deliberately set out to goad Corbett in the hope that it would affect his concentration, but the insults only served to turn the master of scientific defence into a demon of attack and he gave Mitchell a terrible hiding before he was counted out in round three.

After losing to Bob Fitzsimmons in his third defence following a three-year lay-off, Corbett made two attempts to win back the championship against James J. Jeffries but was each time bulldozed to defeat by his stronger, harder-punching opponent.

> You become a champion by fighting one more round. When things are tough, you fight one more round, remembering that the man who always fights one more round is never whipped. In life there's always one more round.

BOB FITZSIMMONS 1897–1899

Born: Helston, Cornwall, 4 June 1862
Died: Chicago, 22 October 1917
Height: 5ft 11.75in
Weight: 11st 8lb (162lb)
Reach: 71.75in
Chest: 41–44in
Fist: 12.5in
Nicknames: Freckled Bob and Ruby Robert
Career span: 1880–1914
Record: 62 fights, 40 wins (32 KOs), 11 losses (eight by KO), ten no decisions, one no contest
Age at which title was won: 35 (45th fight)

PRE-Lennox Lewis claims to Bob Fitzsimmons being the 'only British boxer' to win the world heavyweight championship were on weak ground. He was still a child when taken by his Cornish parents to New Zealand where his father opened a blacksmith's business in Timaru. From his schooldays, Bob helped his father in the forge and developed an immense, heavily muscled upper body that looked somehow out of place on what were spindly, freckled legs.

He never weighed more than a middleweight and with his prematurely balding, ginger hair he gave the appearance of being a physical freak. But he was a phenomenal puncher who could take any man out with a single blow. The Americans didn't take him seriously when he arrived in California at the age of 28 to continue a career that started in Australia. He silenced the sneerers by knocking out Jack 'the Nonpareil' Dempsey to win the world middleweight title in 13 rounds in 1891.

Fitz had already applied for US citizenship when he climbed into the ring against James J. Corbett at Carson

City, Nevada, on St Patrick's Day in 1897. At 35, he was four years older and 20lb lighter than the champion, and he was very much the betting underdog. He was taking a battering from Corbett until he followed the ringside advice of his wife, Rose, who shouted, 'Hit him in the slats, Bob.' This referred to the rib area, and in the 14th round Fitz invented what became known as the 'solar plexus' punch. He switched suddenly to southpaw and threw a straight left that corkscrewed deep into Corbett's stomach and knocked the breath out of him. The champion sank to the canvas fighting for air as the referee counted him out.

Fitz lost the title to James J. Jeffries in his first defence, breaking knuckles on both his hands against the granite-hard challenger who outweighed him by 64lb. He was knocked out in the 11th round and survived until the 13th in a return match. At the age of 41, he became the first man to win three world titles when he captured the light-heavyweight crown.

> I developed my strength working alongside my father in his blacksmith's foundry. As a middleweight I was always having to fight bigger men in the heavyweight division. But I used to say of my heavier opponents, "The bigger they are, the harder they fall."

JAMES J. JEFFRIES 1899–1905
Born: Caroll, Ohio, 15 April 1875
Died: Burbank, California, 3 March 1953
Height: 6ft 2.5in
Weight: 15st 7lb (217lb)
Reach: 76.5in
Chest: 43–48in
Fist: 13.5in
Nicknames: The Boilermaker and Californian
Grizzly Bear
Career span: 1896–1910
Record: 21 fights, 18 wins (15 KOs), one loss, two draws
Age at which title was won: 24 (13th fight)

JAMES J. Jeffries started his boxing career as a sparring partner for James J. Corbett. Gentleman Jim acted in something less than a gentlemanly manner and each day in training used to give the strongly built boilermaker from California via Ohio a painful hiding.

After taking the world heavyweight crown from the outweighed and outgunned Bob Fitzsimmons in 1899, Jeffries gave Corbett two chances to regain the championship. Each time he gained revenge for all the punishment he had taken in training, although he looked on the verge of defeat in their first meeting at Coney Island in 1900. Corbett outboxed and outfoxed him for 23 rounds before being caught by a right that stretched him flat out as he came bouncing off the ropes. In the return in San Francisco in 1903, the old champion ran out of steam after building up an early lead and Jeffries knocked him out in the tenth round.

Trained by former world middleweight champion Tommy Ryan, Jeffries was taught – like Rocky Marciano 50 years later – to fight out of a crouch and his tucked-up style made him a difficult man to pin with any telling punches. The 'Jeffries Crouch' was copied by many fighters of his era, but few could match the champion's success with it.

He defended the title against Tom Sharkey (on points after 25 rounds), Gus Ruhlin (Ruhlin retired after the fifth round) and Jack Munroe (won by knockout in the second round) before announcing his retirement as undefeated champion in 1905. He had won 18 and drawn two of his 20 professional contests.

Six years into his retirement, Jeffries allowed himself to be talked back into the ring for a showdown with Jack Johnson, who was despised by many white American fight fans unable to come to terms with a black man holding the title. Jeffries, as they say in the fight trade, 'shouldda stood in bed'. At 35 and no longer a magnificent physical specimen, he was outclassed by the hugely talented Johnson, who battered him to a standstill in 15 rounds.

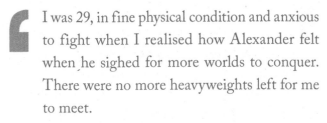

I was 29, in fine physical condition and anxious to fight when I realised how Alexander felt when he sighed for more worlds to conquer. There were no more heavyweights left for me to meet.

This was before he unwisely made a comeback against Jack Johnson.

MARVIN HART 1905–1906

Born: Jefferson County, Kentucky, 16 September 1876
Died: Fern Creek, Kentucky, 17 September 1931
Height: 5ft 11in
Weight: 13st 5lb (187lb)
Reach: 74in
Chest: 45–47in
Fist: 14in
Nickname: Punching Plumber
Career span: 1899–1910
Record: 47 fights, 32 wins (19 KOs), nine losses, six draws
Age at which title was won: 29 (35th fight)

OF all the world heavyweight title holders, Marvin Hart has made the least impact on the public consciousness, mainly because his wore something of a paper crown; but if only for the fact that he was once given a points verdict over the mighty Jack Johnson – 'given' being the operative word – he merits his place in this parade of world heavyweight champions.

Hart, a combative, two-fisted fighter who relied more on strength than skill, became world champion in dubious circumstances. When James J. Jeffries retired undefeated in 1905 the title became vacant. There were two contenders who stood out: Jack Johnson and Sam Langford, but both were ruled out by the boxing establishment because they were black. There was no sport that could match boxing for exposing the cancer of bigotry.

On 28 May 1905, Hart met Johnson in a non-title contest over 20 rounds and was adjudged to have won on points. One ringside boxing reporter summed up the result memorably with the line, 'Hart could only have got the decision owing to the fact that in the excitement the referee pointed to the wrong man.'

Hart then outgunned former world light-heavyweight champion Jack Root at Reno on 5 July 1905 in a fight that the idolised Jeffries was persuaded to describe as for 'my vacant title'. Jeffries was the referee and stopped the fight in Hart's favour in the 12th round.

The son of a family with roots deep in Germany, Hart slipped quickly from the world stage when he lost his title in his first defence against Canadian Tommy Burns in Los Angeles on 23 February 1906. Again, Jim Jeffries was the referee.

Hart retired to a red-shuttered cottage on a small farm in Fern Creek, in his home state of Kentucky, where he combined farming with plumbing. He also became a prominent referee in the wrestling world as well as boxing rings. A burly, affable man, Hart was nicknamed the 'Louisville Plumber', but lacked the gift of the gab of another Louisville fighter who would come along 60 years later. He died of liver problems one day after his 55th birthday.

 All the championship earned me was $10,000. I guess I was born 20 years too soon.

TOMMY BURNS 1906–1908
Born: Chesley, Ontario, 17 June 1881
Died: Vancouver, 10 May 1955
Height: 5ft 7in
Weight: 12st 5lb (173lb)
Reach: 74.5in
Chest: 40–44in
Fist: 12in
Career span: 1900–1920
Record: 60 fights, 46 wins (36 KOs), eight draws, five losses (one by KO), one no decision
Age at which title was won: 25 (42nd fight)

CANADIAN Tommy Burns, at 5ft 7in, was the shortest man ever to win the world heavyweight title and was never more than a light-heavyweight. But he beat a procession of much bigger and more powerful men by nimble footwork, stunningly accurate counter-punching and enormous willpower. Burns (real name Noah Brusso) had an extraordinarily long reach for such a short man and he used to draw opponents in like a spider luring a fly and then knock them senseless with pinpointed punches to the most vulnerable parts of the body.

Self-managed Burns, the thinking man's fighter, became champion in 1906 by winning on points over pretender to the throne Marvin Hart. Burns, an astute businessman, then set about earning as much money as possible while keeping ahead of the feared Jack Johnson, who trailed him around the world throwing out challenges. He successfully defended the title 11 times (including a 20 rounds draw and then a 20 rounds points win over Jack O'Brien) before Johnson finally caught up with him in Sydney, Australia, after chasing him through Europe.

Wise Burns knew he had little chance against the 'Galveston Giant' and demanded and got a record $30,000 purse to put his title on the line on Boxing Day 1908. Johnson made him earn every cent, toying with the champion and hitting him with a stream of insulting words as well as injurious punches before police jumped into the ring and stopped the one-sided savagery in the 14th round.

Burns had six more contests before retiring after a seventh-round defeat by Britain's Joe Beckett in London in 1920. Burns later became an ordained minister, and said, 'Boxing is vicious and full of hatred. My only purpose in life now is to spread universal love. I'm through hurting people.'

> I will defend my title as heavyweight champion of the world against all comers, none barred. By this I mean black, Mexican, Indian or any other nationality without regard to colour, size or nativity. I propose to be the champion of the world, not the white or the Canadian or the American or any other limited degree of champion.

JACK JOHNSON 1908–1915

Born: Galveston, Texas, 31 March 1878
Died: North Carolina, 10 April 1946
Height: 6ft
Weight: 13st 10lb (192lb)
Reach: 74in
Chest: 38–43in
Fist: 14in
Nicknames: Li'l Artha and the Galveston Giant.
Career span: 1897–1928
Record: 113 fights, 79 wins (45 KOs), 12 draws, eight losses (five by KO), 14 no decisions
Age at which title was won: 30 (79th fight)

IT took Jack Johnson ten frustrating years to reach the status of number one challenger for the world heavyweight title in an era when the colour of your skin rather than your ability dictated matters. For at least five years Johnson was the best heavyweight fighter in the world, but most of the leading white heavyweights dodged him by drawing what was known as the 'colour line'.

He chased Tommy Burns halfway around the world before finally catching up with him and relieving him of the title in Australia.

Johnson's victory, coupled with his arrogant manner and controversial lifestyle, made him one of the most unpopular figures in the United States and a massive hunt was launched for a 'white hope' who could dethrone him. World middleweight champion Stanley Ketchel, the 'Michigan Assassin', was persuaded to try his luck and finished with two of his teeth embedded in Johnson's right glove after he had been knocked cold in the 12th round following a punch that briefly put Johnson on the canvas.

Then James J. Jeffries was brought out of retirement and was pounded to a 15th-round defeat. Johnson was the greatest defensive boxer ever seen, and a master at picking off punches with open gloves and then throwing cutting counters.

He stopped 'Fireman' Jim Flynn in nine rounds in Las Vegas and then became exiled in Europe for three years after being accused of 'transporting a white woman for immoral purposes'.

Johnson jumped bail and had three fights in Paris before being talked into defending his title against giant Jess Willard in the open air in Havana in 1915. He was well ahead on points until reaching the edge of exhaustion under the boiling sun and was knocked out in the 26th round. Johnson later claimed that he had deliberately thrown the fight, but film of the contest supports Willard's case that he won fair and square.

Johnson carried on fighting until he was past 50 and right up until his death in a car crash at 68 he was still giving exhibitions.

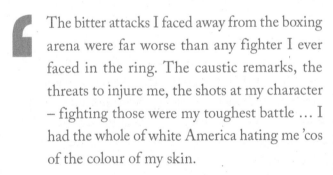

The bitter attacks I faced away from the boxing arena were far worse than any fighter I ever faced in the ring. The caustic remarks, the threats to injure me, the shots at my character – fighting those were my toughest battle ... I had the whole of white America hating me 'cos of the colour of my skin.

JESS WILLARD 1915–1919

Born: Pottawatomie County, Kansas, 29 December 1881
Died: Los Angeles, 15 December 1968
Height: 6ft 6in
Weight: 17st 8lb (246lb)
Reach: 83in
Chest: 46–49.5in
Fist: 14in
Nickname: The Pottawatomie Giant
Career span: 1911–1923
Record: 35 fights, 24 wins (21 KOs), one draw, six losses (three by KO), four no decisions
Age at which title was won: 33 (31st fight)

JUST about everything was taken away from Jess Willard, the fighting cowboy. The glory he should have earned for winning the world title was tarnished by Jack Johnson claims that he had thrown the fight. Then his championship was ripped away by a two-fisted tornado called Jack Dempsey, and unscrupulous managers fleeced him of his hard-earned money. They even tried to take away his lasting place in the record books. It was always believed that at 6ft 6in Willard stood tallest of all the old champions, but a Harvard University professor claimed long after the fighter's death that he could scientifically prove that Willard was in fact a full inch shorter than the promoters had always claimed.

Jess was a manufactured fighter who did not take up boxing until he was 28. What he lacked in skill he made up for in strength and stamina, and he used to wear down rather than outclass his opponents. His colossal reach of 83 inches meant he was able to keep his opponents away merely by sticking out a ramrod left jab.

Willard was manoeuvred into a fight with Jack Johnson because promoter Jack Curley believed it would take a strong rather than a skilful man to beat the 37-year-old champion. The fight was deliberately made over 45 rounds to handicap the veteran Johnson.

After his 26th-round knockout victory, Willard became a hero to white America and he cashed in on his popularity by making a coast-to-coast tour as the main attraction with a travelling circus.

He made a solitary defence, getting the best of Frank Moran in a ten rounds no-decision contest in 1916. Three years later Willard was coaxed into at last climbing into the ring to defend the title against Dempsey, who stopped the giant cowboy in three rounds of legalised brutality. Willard retired, and then in 1923 made a comeback against the 'Wild Bull of the Pampas', Luis Ángel Firpo, who hammered him to an eighth-round defeat.

> In the first round when Dempsey hit me with a left hook, I tried hard to continue, but I was rapidly losing my strength. My eye closed tight and I realised that it would be useless for me to continue, as I could hardly see. It was hard to admit defeat, but Dempsey is the hardest puncher I ever faced.

JACK DEMPSEY 1919–1926
Born: Manassa, Colorado, 24 June 1895
Died: New York, 31 May 1983
Height: 6ft 1in
Weight: 13st 4lb (186lb)
Reach: 77in
Chest: 42–46in
Fist: 11in
Nicknames: Manassa Mauler and Idol of Fistiana
Career span: 1914–1940
Record: 81 fights, 60 wins (49 KOs), eight draws, seven losses (one by KO), six no decisions
Age at which title was won: 24 (73rd fight)

THERE has been no more exciting and explosive heavyweight champion than William Harrison Dempsey, who took his ring name from a former middleweight hero. Dempsey, who had great charisma to go with his devastating power, rose from bar-room brawler and hobo to become one of the most famous and feted sportsmen in history.

After a string of unrecorded fights under the name of Kid Blackie, Dempsey teamed up with manager and publicist Jack 'Doc' Kearns. With Kearns beating the publicity drum and Dempsey beating all the opposition, the Manassa Mauler forced himself into championship contention and tore the title away from Jess Willard in three rounds.

Kearns was so confident that Dempsey would crush Willard that he bet the entire $27,500 purse at odds of 10/1 that he would win in the first round. Dempsey dropped the hulking cowboy seven times, but the bell saved Willard and so Dempsey didn't earn a cent. But six successful title defences turned him into a millionaire before he lost the title to Gene Tunney in 1926.

Dempsey was the first fighter to attract a $1m gate when he knocked out gallant Frenchman Georges Carpentier in four rounds in 1921, and his second title battle with Tunney in 1927 drew the first $2m gate.

Jolting Jack's championship clash with Argentinian Luis Ángel Firpo was labelled the most thrilling fight of all time – and it was all over within two rounds.

Firpo was flattened seven times in the opening round and then somehow found the strength to knock Dempsey through the ropes and out of the ring. The champion was pushed back in by press men just before the bell. Dempsey tamed the Wild Bull of the Pampas by knocking him out in the second round.

He was weighed down with worries of lawsuits and domestic problems when he lost his world title in his next defence against Tunney.

> You know what a champion is? A champion is someone who's ready when the bell rings – not just before, not just after – but when it rings …
> A champion owes everybody something. He can never pay back for all the help he got, for making him an idol.

GENE TUNNEY 1926–1928
Born: New York City, 25 May 1898
Died: Greenwich, Connecticut, 7 November 1978
Height: 6ft 1in
Weight: 13st 5lb (187lb)
Reach: 77in
Chest: 42–45in
Fist: 11in
Nickname: The Fighting Marine
Career span: 1915–1928
Record: 77 fights, 57 wins (42 KOs), one draw, one loss,
17 no decisions, one no contest
Age at which title was won: 28 (75th fight)

GENE Tunney was the most calculating of all the heavyweight champions. Everybody was convinced that Dempsey was unbeatable, but Tunney knew he could be mastered with the right tactics. He considered boxing the Noble Art and perfected and polished his skills in the gymnasium and always made a close study of his opponents.

It was in the US Marines during the First World War that he first came to prominence as an outstanding ring technician while boxing as a light-heavyweight. Shakespeare-quoting Tunney out-thought all his opponents, and after reversing his one and only defeat by Harry 'Smash and Grab' Greb, he campaigned to challenge for Dempsey's crown. They finally met in a rainstorm in Philadelphia on 23 September 1926, and Tunney cleverly boxed on the retreat to win an undisputed points victory.

Tunney gave Dempsey a revenge chance a year later in Chicago and came perilously close to losing the title in the famous 'Battle of the Long Count'. Dempsey dropped Tunney in the seventh round and hovered over the dazed champion, ignoring the referee's instructions to go to a neutral corner. By the time Tunney was back on his unsteady feet, 14 seconds had ticked away. The New Yorker danced away from further trouble and repeated his ten-round points victory. The champion always maintained that he could have got up before the ten-second count if it had been necessary, and the referee said that Dempsey had only himself to blame for not immediately abiding by the new rules and going to a neutral corner.

Tunney successfully defended the title once more against New Zealander Tom Heeney in New York City on 26 July 1928. The fight did not capture the public imagination and promoter Tex Rickard lost $150,000. After stopping Heeney in 11 rounds, Tunney married a wealthy heiress and retired from the ring with his hero status undiminished.

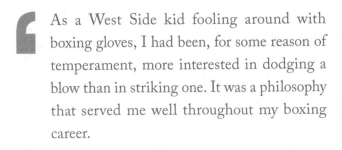

> As a West Side kid fooling around with boxing gloves, I had been, for some reason of temperament, more interested in dodging a blow than in striking one. It was a philosophy that served me well throughout my boxing career.

MAX SCHMELING 1930–1932

Born: Klein Luckow, Brandenburg, Germany, 28
September 1905
Died: Wenzendorf, Germany, 2 February 2005
Height: 6ft 1in
Weight: 13st 4lb (186lb)
Reach: 76in
Chest: 43–47in
Fist: 12in
Nickname: Black Uhlan
Career span: 1924–1948
Record: 70 fights, 56 wins (38 KOs), four draws, ten
losses (five by KO)
Age at which title was won: 24 (50th fight)

MAX Schmeling became the only champion to win the world heavyweight title while on the canvas. He was put there by a low punch from Jack Sharkey in the fourth round of a 1930 championship contest to find a successor to the throne vacated by Gene Tunney. Within seconds, Schmeling's voluble manager Joe Jacobs was up on the ring apron demanding that the referee disqualify Sharkey. Eventually the official, Jim Crowley, reluctantly agreed to the demands of Jacobs after consulting the two ringside judges – much to the disgust and anger of the near-80,000 crowd at Yankee Stadium in New York.

This did not make Schmeling the most popular of champions, particularly as he became the first fighter to take the heavyweight crown away from North America (Bob Fitzsimmons adopted American citizenship). Schmeling proved his ability a year later by stopping the highly rated Young Stribling – 'the Pride of Georgia' – in the last seconds of a 15-round title defence. The champion was then pressed into giving Sharkey a return at Long Island on 21 June 1932, and lost a narrow points verdict and the title.

The beetle-browed German had his most famous victory to come. Promoter Mike Jacobs fed Schmeling to the up-and-coming Joe Louis, who had been a winner of all his 27 fights. Schmeling, now a cagey veteran of 31, grounded the Brown Bomber with his favourite straight right in the fourth round and finally knocked him out in the 12th. This victory by Schmeling was later avenged by Louis with a devastating first-round knockout in a fight in which racial hatred poisoned the atmosphere because of Hitler's doctrine.

During the war, Schmeling – as punishment by the Nazis for losing to Louis – served as a paratrooper and was wounded at the Battle of Crete. He made a brief comeback in 1947 and then retired to run a mink farm, and he also had the lucrative franchise to distribute Coca-Cola in Germany, which turned him into a millionaire.

Max died in his homeland seven months short of his 100th birthday.

> 'Looking back, I'm almost happy I lost that title fight with Louis. Just imagine if I'd have come back to Germany with a victory. I had nothing to do with the Nazis, but they would have given me an Iron Cross and fed on my status as world champion. After the war I might have been considered a war criminal.'

JACK SHARKEY 1932–1933

Born: Binghampton, New York, 6 October 1902
Died: Epping, New Hampshire, 21 August 1994
Height: 6ft
Weight: 14st 6lb (202lb)
Reach: 74in
Chest: 40–45in
Fist: 12in
Nicknames: Boston Gob and Sobbing Sailor
Career span: 1924–1936
Record: 55 fights, 38 wins (14 KOs), three draws, 13 losses (four by KO), one no decision
Age at which title was won: 29 (47th fight)

LOW blows played a prominent part in the career of Jack Sharkey, a Lithuanian-blooded fighter whose real name was Joseph Zukauskas. He won the right to meet Max Schmeling for the vacant world championship by beating British champion Phil Scott in an eliminator with a punch that was unquestionably below the belt.

Sharkey, who had been in the US Navy, started his professional career while still a seaman. He made such rapid progress that he was matched with Jack Dempsey as a warm-up for the Manassa Mauler's second fight with Gene Tunney.

In most of his previous contests, Sharkey had managed to tie up his opponents with clever use of the ring, but Dempsey knocked him cold in the seventh round. Ironically, the knockout blow landed while Sharkey was turning towards the referee to protest about an alleged low blow.

After being disqualified for a low punch in his first fight with Schmeling, Sharkey earned another crack at the new champion by outpointing giant Italian Primo Carnera. He won the return bout against Schmeling on a split points decision over 15 rounds to become world champion.

His first title defence was against Carnera at Long Island on 29 June 1933. Even Carnera seemed surprised when a right uppercut dropped Sharkey to the canvas for the full count in round six. It was a 'mystery' punch to rival that of the Muhammad Ali blow that knocked out Sonny Liston nearly 30 years later.

Few at the ringside saw the punch and the claims of Sharkey's handlers that Carnera had a weight hidden in his glove were laughed off. During a comeback campaign three years later, Sharkey was talked into testing the young Joe Louis. The former sailor was all at sea against the Brown Bomber and was knocked out in the third round. He retired to become a champion fly cast fisherman, and lived to the ripe old age of 91.

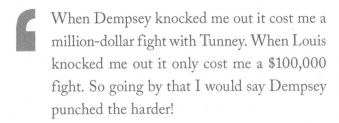

When Dempsey knocked me out it cost me a million-dollar fight with Tunney. When Louis knocked me out it only cost me a $100,000 fight. So going by that I would say Dempsey punched the harder!

PRIMO CARNERA 1933–1934

Born: Sequals, Italy, 26 October 1906
Died: Sequals, 29 June 1967
Height: 6ft 5in
Weight: 18st 6lb (258lb)
Reach: 85in
Chest: 48–54in
Fist: 14in
Nickname: The Ambling Alp
Career span: 1928–1945
Record: 103 fights, 88 wins (69 KOs), 14 losses (five by KO), one no contest
Age at which title was won: 26 (82nd fight)

PRIMO Carnera, a former circus strongman, had the saddest career of any world heavyweight champion. Because of his gigantic size, he was paraded around the boxing rings of the world as some sort of freak by managers who fleeced him and left him wrecked and destitute. In the days when he was being looked after properly, he came to Britain in 1930 and was trained by the famous Gutteridge twins for a fight against British champion Reggie Meen that he won by a second-round knockout.

It was when he moved to the US that the leeches closed in and bled him dry. After beating a string of carefully chosen opponents, he became a box office attraction and emerged as a contender for the world title by stopping Ernie Schaaf in 13 rounds. Tragically, Schaaf died after the contest and Carnera had to face a commission before he was exonerated.

The simple but likeable Italian – known to be 'Mob' ruled – challenged Jack Sharkey for the title at Long Island on 29 June 1933, and won the crown with a sixth-round knockout blow that became known as one of the phantom punches of boxing because few saw it.

Despite his clumsy, lumbering style that earned him his 'Ambling Alp' nickname, Carnera was an accomplished boxer with a solid left jab and a ponderous but damaging right cross. He made successful title defences against Paulino Uzcudun and Tommy Loughran before losing the championship to Max Baer in the 11th round of their 1934 title fight.

Like so many of his contemporaries, Carnera was battered by the superior Joe Louis and disappeared from the title picture. Once his days as a meal ticket were over, all the hangers-on left him. He later found self-respect and money that he could hang on to by becoming a successful professional wrestler. After his retirement, he ran (and tried to drink dry) a liquor store in Los Angeles before returning to his birthplace of Sequals for the last months of his life. He was given a national hero's funeral.

 I was a humble carpenter, and I became heavyweight champion of the world. I did good.

MAX BAER 1934–1935
Born: Omaha, Nebraska, 11 February 1909
Died: Hollywood, California, 21 November 1959
Height: 6ft 2in
Weight: 15st (210lb)
Reach: 81in
Chest: 44–47in
Fist: 12in
Nicknames: The Livermore Larruper and Madcap Maxie
Career span: 1929–1941
Record: 83 fights, 70 wins (52 KOs), 13 losses
(three by KO)
Age at which title was won: 25 (47th fight)

MAX Baer could and would have been one of the greatest champions of the 1930s if only he had been able to take boxing – and life – more seriously. The thing Baer lacked was dedication. He was an unashamed playboy ('Give me broads before boxing any day') and was continually clowning, both in and out of the ring.

During the first round of his rough-and-tumble title fight with Primo Carnera, champion and challenger fell to the canvas in an untidy heap. Baer patted a bewildered Carnera on the backside and said, 'Last one up's a sissy.' Poor old Primo wasn't laughing in the 11th round when the referee stopped the fight after he had been down for the 11th time in a farcical brawl that did little for the status of world heavyweight championship boxing.

Baer amazingly managed to lose the the title exactly a year later, on 13 June 1935, to 10/1 underdog James J. Braddock. Few people gave Braddock a chance but the casual, complacent Baer completely underestimated him and hardly bothered to train for the contest. He laughed and shrugged off his stunning points defeat. 'Jimmy's only borrowed the title – I'll get it back,' he said. But three months later, his hopes of recapturing the crown were exploded when he became the latest slaughter victim for Joe Louis, who knocked him out in four rounds, despite the corner advice that Max was getting from former champion Jack Dempsey.

His younger brother, Buddy, twice tried to regain the championship for the Baer family, but was each time destroyed by the lethal Louis. Clowning Max, one of the hardest right-hand punchers of all time, then had a losing and a winning fight against Britain's Tommy Farr and boxed on until joining the US Army in 1942. He later followed a career as an actor and entertainer in Hollywood, where he died of a heart attack at the age of 50. His son, Max Jr., starred as Jethro in the long-running TV comedy *The Beverly Hillbillies.*

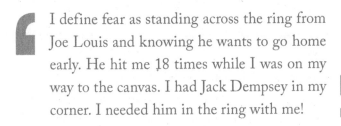

I define fear as standing across the ring from Joe Louis and knowing he wants to go home early. He hit me 18 times while I was on my way to the canvas. I had Jack Dempsey in my corner. I needed him in the ring with me!

JAMES J. BRADDOCK 1935–1937
Born: New York City, 6 December 1905
Died: New Jersey, 29 November 1974
Height: 6ft 2in
Weight: 13st 8lb (190lb)
Reach: 75in
Chest: 41–44in
Fist: 11.5in
Nickname: Cinderella Man
Career span: 1926–1938
Record: 86 fights, 46 wins (27 KOs), four draws, 23 losses
(two by KO), 11 no decisions, two no contests
Age at which title was won: 29 (84th fight)

JAMES J. Braddock became affectionately known as the
Cinderella Man because he arrived so late for the brawl. A
29-year-old dockworker, he had been on the breadline in the
Depression years and was in semi-retirement when he got
his world championship chance and astonished everybody
by taking the title from Max Baer at Long Island on 13
June 1935.

Suddenly the disbelieving world had a heavyweight
champion who had won only 46 of his previous 83 contests.
Braddock, who had boxed mainly as a middleweight and
light-heavyweight, had failed in a bid for the light-heavy
title in 1929, when he was outpointed by Tommy Loughran.
He was a smart, orthodox boxer but lacked the punching
power to make a really big impact in the heavyweight
division – that is, until he got his opportunity against Baer,
following an impressive points victory over long-time world
light-heavyweight champion John Henry Lewis.

With the champion less than fully committed to the
fight, Braddock produced the performance of a lifetime to
outbox and outgeneral the lacklustre Livermore Larruper.

He boxed on the retreat and never gave Baer the chance to set himself for his big right hand punch. At the end of 15 rounds he was voted a unanimous points winner and the new king of the world heavyweights.

He should have met Max Schmeling in his first defence but was bribed into putting his title on the line against Joe Louis by being guaranteed ten per cent of his challenger's future purses as title-holder if the championship changed hands.

Despite briefly flooring Louis for a two-count in the first round, Braddock was no match for his young challenger who blasted him to defeat in eight rounds. Braddock had one more winning fight – a points victory over Welsh hero Tommy Farr – and then retired. His money, boosted by his cut of the Joe Louis purses, was wisely invested and he became a wealthy businessman – a far cry from when he queued up for handouts to help feed his wife and three children.

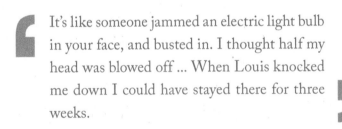

It's like someone jammed an electric light bulb in your face, and busted in. I thought half my head was blowed off ... When Louis knocked me down I could have stayed there for three weeks.

JOE LOUIS 1937–1949
Born: Lafayette, Alabama, 13 May 1914
Died: Las Vegas, Nevada, 12 April 1981
Height: 6ft 1.5in
Weight: 14st 2lb (198lb)
Reach: 76in
Chest: 42–45in
Fist: 11.75in
Nickname: Brown Bomber
Career span: 1934–1951
Record: 70 fights, 67 wins (53 KOs), three losses
(two by KO)
Age at which title was won: 23 (36th fight)

JOE Louis was the complete champion. He was a composed and clever boxer, carried a knockout punch in either hand, was a skilled craftsman and had strength and courage. The only opponent he could never beat was the tax man, and he finished up broke at the end of a career in which his ring earnings totalled $5m.

There was only one scar on the Louis record when he captured the championship by knocking out James J. Braddock in eight rounds in Chicago on 22 June 1937. But he soon reversed this one setback by smashing Max Schmeling to a sensational one-round defeat a year to the day after becoming champion.

Louis survived a close call against brave Welshman Tommy Farr on the way to a record 25 successful title defences. He was champion – a great champion – for 12 years, overcoming all challengers during what became famous as his 'Bum A Month' campaign.

After winning two memorable battles with Jersey Joe Walcott, Louis announced his retirement from the ring in March 1949. The Brown Bomber was grounding himself as undefeated champion. Sadly, his story does not end there. His tax troubles ran so deep that he was forced into making a comeback within two years and failed in a bid to regain the title from the skilled and strong Ezzard Charles.

Though a shuffling shadow of his former self, he was allowed to be put up for slaughter against a rising young hurricane of a heavyweight called Rocky Marciano. The fight produced one of the saddest sights in sporting history, Louis being pounded through the ropes and stopped in eight one-sided rounds.

'I couldn't bring myself to count Joe out, so I stopped the fight,' said referee Ruby Goldstein, capturing the supreme status that Louis had in boxing. Joe always carried himself with great dignity both inside and outside the ring and there has never been a more respected champion in sporting history. In later years he had a drug habit and domestic problems, but this was not allowed to damage his standing as a hero for all seasons.

 When I was boxing I made five million bucks and wound up broke, owing the government a million. It was like carrying a boulder on my back. I was a boxer, not an accountant.

EZZARD CHARLES 1949–1951

Born: Lawrenceville, Georgia, 7 July 1921
Died: Chicago, 27 May 1970
Height: 6ft
Weight: 13st (182lb)
Reach: 74in
Chest: 39–42in
Fist: 12in
Nickname: Cincinnati Cobra
Career span: 1940–1959
Record: 122 fights, 96 wins (58 KOs), one draw, 25 losses (seven by KO)
Age at which title was won: 29 (74th fight)

EZZARD Charles was never the most popular of champions, mainly because he did the unforgiveable thing of beating the legend that was Joe Louis.

Charles had turned professional at 18 in 1940 after winning all of his 42 amateur contests including the Golden Gloves final. He first of all campaigned as a light-heavyweight, beating Archie Moore and Joey Maxim three times each, and then moved up to the heavyweight division and captured the title relinquished by Louis in 1949 by outpointing Jersey Joe Walcott.

The Brown Bomber, weighed down by financial problems, changed his mind about retiring and challenged Charles for the title that the public still considered Joe's property. The fight was staged on 27 September 1950 in New York, and Charles scored a points victory over a man who was just a shambling shadow of a once-great champion.

Charles, a stylish fighter with fast fists and a solid defence, successfully defended the title eight times in two years before running into a classic left hook in the seventh round of a third title clash with Walcott. He was outpointed by his old adversary Walcott when he tried to regain the championship and in 1954 lost two bruising title battles with Rocky Marciano.

Ezzard, who never scaled more than a few pounds above the light-heavyweight limit, was skilful enough to take Marciano 15 rounds in their first meeting but was knocked out in the eighth round of their return after inflicting a serious nose injury on Rocky that was to hurry Marciano's retirement from boxing.

In all Charles took part in 13 world title contests yet somehow managed to wind up broke and bitter, hanging up his gloves at the age of 38 when he started being beaten by opponents who would not have been able to hit his shadow when he was at his peak. He finished up in a wheelchair suffering from a form of multiple sclerosis. Ezzard is remembered as a fine all-round ring technician, who was unlucky to live in the shadow of Joe Louis and then stand in the path of a hurricane called Marciano.

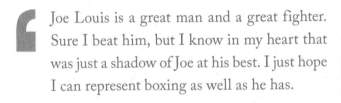

Joe Louis is a great man and a great fighter. Sure I beat him, but I know in my heart that was just a shadow of Joe at his best. I just hope I can represent boxing as well as he has.

JERSEY JOE WALCOTT 1951–1952
Born: Merchantville, New Jersey, 31 January 1914
Died: Camden, New Jersey, 25 February 1994
Height: 6ft
Weight: 13st 8lb (190lb)
Reach: 74in
Chest: 40–43in
Fist: 12in
Nickname: Jersey Joe
Career span: 1930–1953
Record: 69 fights, 50 wins (30 KOs), one draw, 18 losses (six by KO)
Age at which title was won: 37 (66th fight)

JERSEY Joe Walcott became, at 37 years six months, the oldest man to win the world heavyweight title (until the second coming of George Foreman) when he knocked out Ezzard Charles with a cracking left hook in the seventh round of their 1951 title fight.

It had been a long, hard haul to the top of the mountain for Walcott, who had started out in life as Arnold Cream. He borrowed his ring name from a renowned former world welterweight champion.

Jersey Joe, a God-fearing man who always carried a Bible with him outside the ring, had been a hungry fighter in the truest sense. He had a wife and six children to feed.

Walcott had lied about his age so that he could launch his professional career at barely 15, and he had been swindled so many times by unscrupulous managers and promoters that he kept giving up boxing in disgust.

His hungriest years were between 1938 and 1945 when he had just seven fights and he went on the dole to pay the food bills. One freezing cold evening in the winter of 1945 Walcott was visited at his Jersey home by a boxing manager called Felix Bocchicchio, who wanted Joe to sign with him. Walcott pointed to an empty coal bin in the corner of his living room and said, 'Mister, if you can keep that bin full for me I will fight for you.' Over the next eight years Walcott earned enough to buy a coal mine.

He took part in eight world title fights, including two with Joe Louis and four with Ezzard Charles. He was a crafty and shifty box-fighter, bewildering opponents with clever footwork and feints, and he had the punching power to finish fights with one well-executed blow and was particularly successful with his potent left hook.

His brief reign as world champion ended when he came up against a human destroyer by the name of Rocky Marciano. Gentle and genial outside the ring, he later became a referee – remembered for getting flummoxed during the second Ali–Liston title fight.

> I liked that world title, and didn't want to lose it to nobody. But if I was gonna lose it to anybody, I'm glad it was Rocky Marciano. He is a good man, a good fighter and he will be a great champ.

ROCKY MARCIANO 1952–1955

Born: Brockton, Mass., 1 September 1923
Died: Newton, Iowa, 31 August 1969
Height: 5ft 10in
Weight: 13st 2lb (184lb)
Reach: 68in
Chest: 39–42in
Fist: 11in
Nickname: Brockton Blockbuster
Career span: 1947–1955
Record: 49 fights, 49 wins (43 KOs)
Age at which title was won: 29 (43rd fight)

ROCKY used his fists as if they were sledgehammers and he launched his clubbing attacks in such a brutal manner that he was called the '20th-Century Caveman'. Marciano's rise to fame and fortune was like something out of a Hollywood movie. Come to think of it, they could have called his life story *Rocky*!

He was born Rocco Marchegiano in Brockton, Massachusetts, the eldest of six children of immigrant Italian parents who lived on the poverty line. After a brief amateur career, Rocky hitch-hiked to New York for a gymnasium trial under the all-knowing gaze of Madison Square Garden matchmaker Al Weill, who noted Rocky's raw power and had the vision to realise he could be moulded into a fearsome force. He put him under the wing of trainer Charley Goldman, an old-time bantamweight who knew every boxing trick in the book and a few that never quite got into print.

Rocky did not have the ideal build. His fists were small and his reach at 68in the shortest of any world champion. But the tale of the tape doesn't give the overall picture of a man who simply oozed menace. Neither does it record that Rocky had the physical strength of a weightlifter and a granite-tough jaw.

Goldman turned Rocky's short stature to his advantage by having him fight out of a crouch. He was totally dedicated to his training and there has rarely been a fitter fighting machine. After battering an aged, over-the-hill Joe Louis to an eight-round defeat, he tore the world title away from Jersey Joe Walcott with a 13th-round knockout victory in his 43rd fight on 23 September 1952. He knocked Walcott out in the first round in a return match and successfully defended his crown against Ezzard Charles (twice), Roland LaStarza, Britain's Don Cockell (crudely clubbed to a ninth-round defeat) and Archie Moore before retiring as the only undefeated world heavyweight champion in history.

He tragically died in an air crash the day before his 46th birthday after starting a new career as a TV presenter. Rocky was notoriously miserly throughout his career and he died with at least $2m he earned hidden away in shoeboxes and behind false ceilings. Nobody has ever owned up to finding his fortune!

 There is no better feeling than walking down the street knowing you are the heavyweight champion of the world.

FLOYD PATTERSON 1956–1959; 1960–1962
Born: Waco, North Carolina, 4 January 1935
Died: New Paltz, New York, 11 May 2006
Height: 5ft 11in
Weight: 13st 2lb (184lb)
Reach: 71in
Chest: 40–42in
Fist: 12in
Nickname: Freudian Floyd
Career span: 1952–1972
Record: 64 fights, 55 wins (40 KOs), one draw, eight losses (five by KO)
Age at which title was first won: 21 (32nd fight)

FLOYD Patterson, guided by the cagey Cus D'Amato, followed Rocky Marciano as world heavyweight champion when he knocked out 'Ageless' Archie Moore in five rounds in a fight for the vacant title on 30 November 1956. At 21 years and 11 months he was then the youngest heavyweight champion of all time.

The 1952 Olympic middleweight champion, he had fast fists and a distinctive style, launching sudden two-handed attacks from behind a high guard that became known as his 'peek-a-boo' method. He did not have the best of physiques for what was to become the era of the super-heavyweights and he adopted risky attacking tactics in a bid to make up for his lack of weight and reach. He would lunge forward with both feet off the ground in an effort to get maximum power into his punches, but it meant he often left himself open to counter blows and in seven of his 13 title bouts he was knocked down 16 times.

The sagacious D'Amato rarely allowed Patterson into the ring with legitimate contenders and he steered Floyd through successful defences against Tommy Jackson, Pete

Rademacher (the 1956 Olympic champion making his professional debut), Roy Harris and Britain's Brian London, who hardly made an aggressive move before being knocked out in the 11th round.

Then Floyd's world was turned upside down when he underestimated European champion Ingemar Johansson and was stopped in three rounds.

Patterson created history by becoming the first heavyweight champion to regain the title but his 'bogeyman' was waiting around the corner for him in the menacing shape of Sonny Liston.

After twice being shattered inside a round by Liston, Patterson made unsuccessful bids to regain the title for a second time against first Muhammad Ali and then Jimmy Ellis. 'Freudian Floyd' ironed out his psychological problems after retiring and gave a lot back to the game he served with such distinction as a New York boxing commissioner. He also managed his adopted son Tracy. His last years were lost in a maze of dementia.

> People always point out that I was the world heavyweight champion knocked down the most – but I also got up the most.

INGEMAR JOHANSSON 1959–1960

Born: Gothenburg, Sweden, 22 September 1932
Died: Kungsbacka, Sweden, 30 January 2009
Height: 6ft
Weight: 14st (196lb)
Reach: 72in
Chest: 43–45in
Fist: 13in
Nickname: Ingo's Bingo, in reference to his right-hand punch
Career span: 1952–1963
Record: 28 fights, 26 wins (17 KOs), two losses (two by KO)
Age at which title was won: 26 (22nd fight)

THERE has never been a world heavyweight champion quite like 'Swedebasher' Ingemar Johansson. He was an intelligent, handsome man with a big dimple in his chin, and he had a winning smile. Nothing was ever allowed to stop him enjoying the good life, and he led a playboy existence even when training for major fights. It was the norm for him to go nightclubbing and dancing into the early hours during the build-up for title fights, and his beautiful 'secretary' Birgit – later his wife – used to stay with him at his training camps.

Ingo cleverly and craftily exaggerated his playboy image while in the United States preparing for his title shot against Floyd Patterson, and he duped the press and Patterson into thinking he was more interested in fun than fighting. He didn't look a class fighter in the ring, but there was a procession of battered heavyweights in Europe – including Henry Cooper and Joe Erskine – who could vouch for the fact that he was much better than he looked. They had all felt the weight of 'Ingo's Bingo' – his 'goodnight' right that could put anybody to sleep.

His left jab seemed nothing more than a pawing punch, but in actual fact it was an important range-finder for what he called his 'Hammer of Thor', a right-hand punch that was absolutely lethal.

Johansson exploded the punch on Patterson's jaw in the third round of their title fight in New York on 26 June 1959, and Floyd was up and down like a yo-yo seven times before he was finally rescued by referee Ruby Goldstein.

Patterson beat Ingo in two more fights over the following two years when they tied up the world championship, much to the anger of a string of contenders.

Ingemar, who had been disqualified in the 1952 Olympic final for allegedly not giving his best, beat Joe Bygraves, Dick Richardson and Brian London in a brief comeback, but he was saved from a knockout defeat by the final bell against London and he decided there and then to pack in his distinguished career during which he was beaten only by Patterson.

He took part in the New York Marathon with Floyd in 1982, and ran a hotel in Florida before becoming a long-term victim of Alzheimer's.

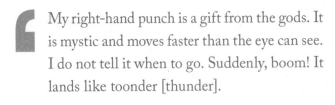

My right-hand punch is a gift from the gods. It is mystic and moves faster than the eye can see. I do not tell it when to go. Suddenly, boom! It lands like toonder [thunder].

SONNY LISTON 1962–1964

Born: Sand Slough, Arkansas, 8 May 1932
Died: Las Vegas, Nevada, 30 December 1970
Height: 6ft 1in
Weight: 15st 3lb (213lb)
Reach: 84in
Chest: 44–46in
Fist: 15in
Nickname: Old Stone Face
Career span: 1953–1970
Record: 54 fights, 50 wins (39 KOs), four losses
(three by KO)
Age at which title was won: 30 (35th fight)

CHARLES 'Sonny' Liston was the meanest, moodiest and also the most mysterious world heavyweight champion of all time. And in the end he finished up as the most tragic of all the champions. Liston started life right at the bottom of the heap. He was one of 25 children fathered during two marriages by Tobe Liston, a poverty-stricken Arkansas farmer.

Liston ran away from home when he was 13 and started a life on the wrong side of the law. He was continually in trouble with the police and it was while serving a five-year prison sentence for robbery that he began to take an interest in boxing. He was paroled in 1952, and after winning a Golden Gloves title he turned professional in 1953.

He won 14 of his first 15 fights and his career was just taking off in a big way when he got involved in an argument with a policeman over a parking ticket. The policeman finished up in hospital with a broken leg. Liston finished up back in prison. He made his comeback after 20 months out of the ring on 29 January 1958 and took his winning record to 33 out of 34 fights.

There were several investigations into Liston's gangster connections and it was with some reluctance that he was given the go-ahead to challenge Floyd Patterson for the world title in Chicago in 1962. A powerhouse of a fighter, Liston flattened Floyd inside one round and gave a repeat performance when they met again the following year.

Liston looked just about unbeatable but then tamely surrendered the championship to chatterboxer Cassius Clay, retiring at the end of six rounds with a claimed shoulder injury.

There was an even deeper mystery 15 months later when Clay (by then Muhammad Ali) knocked him out with a phantom punch in the first round.

Liston won 14 out of 15 fights over the next five years, but was then found dead in his Las Vegas apartment on New Year's Eve in 1970. He was said to have died of natural causes but there were strong rumours that enigmatic Liston had been 'eliminated' by gangster associates. Sad Sonny took his secrets with him to the grave.

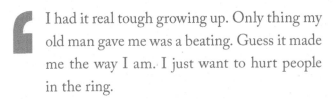 I had it real tough growing up. Only thing my old man gave me was a beating. Guess it made me the way I am. I just want to hurt people in the ring.

CASSIUS CLAY/MUHAMMAD ALI 1964–1967; 1974–1978

Born: Louisville, Kentucky, 17 January 1942
Died: Scottsdale, Arizona, 3 June 2016
Name at birth: Cassius Marcellus Clay
Height: 6ft 3in
Weight: 15st 10lb (220lb)
Reach: 82in
Chest: 43–45in
Fist: 12in
Nicknames: Louisville Lip and The Greatest
Career span: 1960–1981
Record: 61 fights, 56 wins (37 KOs), five losses
(stopped once)
Age at which title was first won: 22 (20th fight)

BOXING has always attracted colourful, controversial and entertaining characters but they would all have to bow the knee to Muhammad Ali as the greatest sporting showman of the 20th century. He transcended sport and his face – and voice – became just about the best known in the world.

The descendant of a slave and the son of a Kentucky sign writer, he had three boxing careers in one. First there was the brash, flash gaseous Cassius Clay who after winning the 1960 Olympic light-heavyweight gold medal was launched as a professional and was dubbed the 'Louisville Lip' as he drummed up box-office business with a tongue that was even quicker than his fast fists.

In his early fights he gave poetic and prophetic forecasts of the round in which he would win, and he was rarely wrong. 'Moore will fall in four' was typical. He survived a fourth-round knock-down against Henry Cooper on the way to 19 victories and a title challenge against 'big, bad' Sonny Liston.

Following two dramatic victories over Liston, he dropped his slave name of Clay and started the second phase of his career with the Muslim name Muhammad Ali. He made ten winning title defences before being stripped of the championship in 1967 for refusing to join the US Army on religious grounds.

The third stage of his extraordinary career came after a three-and-a-half-year lay-off and he regained his title with an incredible eighth-round knockout victory over George Foreman in Zaire in 1974, the famous 'Rumble in the Jungle'.

He again defended the title ten times before losing it to Leon Spinks, whom he outpointed in a return to become the first man in history to win the heavyweight crown three times.

Ali went to the well several times too often and was stopped for the only time when he retired at the end of ten rounds against Larry Holmes in 1980. He avenged three of the five defeats in his 21-year career (by Joe Frazier, Ken Norton and Spinks) and his setbacks against Holmes and Trevor Berbick came long after he should have dropped the curtain on perhaps the greatest boxing career of all time.

Sadly, he was afflicted by Parkinson's disease in retirement, and became a shuffling shadow of the man who had been the Great Entertainer.

 I am The Greatest.

LEON SPINKS 1978
Born: St Louis, Missouri, 11 July 1953
Died: Henderson, Nevada, 5 February 2021
Height: 6ft 1in
Weight: 15st (210lb)
Reach: 76in
Chest: 40–43in
Fist: 12in
Nickname: Neon Leon
Career span: 1977–1995
Record: 46 fights, 26 wins (14 KOs), 17 losses (nine by KO), three draws
Age at which title was won: 24 (eighth fight)

LEON and Michael Spinks created ring history by becoming the first brothers to win Olympic titles in the 1976 Games in Montreal. Leon, the light-heavyweight champion, was then rushed with indecent haste into a title fight with Muhammad Ali after only seven professional fights, six of which he won with one drawn.

'Neon Leon' caused one of the boxing shocks of the century by outpointing Ali in Las Vegas on 15 February 1978. Those cynics who considered it a set-up result could not have seen Ali in the dressing room after the fight, with swollen features and a painful gash inside his mouth. He had looked on the verge of exhaustion at the finish of the fight after he traded punches with the younger man in a last round of earthquaking excitement and bravery as he went all out for a title-saving knockout.

Ali took his defeat in dignified manner, without acrimony or alibis. 'No complaints,' he said. 'Leon is a fine young fighter and deserved his victory. Now I have the motivation to win the title for a third time. I will come again.'

Leon only had the title on loan. Ali outpointed him in the return in New Orleans seven months later to win the crown for a record third time. Because he preferred a return fight with Ali to a mandatory defence against Ken Norton, Spinks was stripped of his WBC title before the rematch.

The victory over Ali by ex-Marine Spinks was his peak performance. He was never able to cope with the pressures and fame that come hand in hand with the world title. He had problems with drugs and seemed doomed to disappear back into the ghetto from which boxing had briefly released him.

Bombed to defeats by Gerrie Coetzee and Larry Holmes, he made several attempts at a comeback, and he hit rock bottom when he was knocked out in the first round by an opponent making his professional debut.

His son, Cory – born five days after he beat Ali – became world welterweight champion in 2002. Another son, 19-year-old Leon, was shot dead in an unsolved murder in 1990. Spinks was diagnosed with brain damage in 2012 and died of cancer in 2021 aged 67.

 I'm livin' the dream. It don't get better than this.

JOE FRAZIER 1968–1973

Born: Beaufort, South Carolina, 12 January 1944
Died: Philadelphia, Pennsylvania, 7 November 2011
Height: 5ft 11.5in
Weight: 14st 7lb (203lb)
Reach: 73in
Chest: 42–44in
Fist: 13in
Nickname: Smokin' Joe
Career span: 1965–1981
Record: 37 fights, 32 wins (27 KOs), one draw, four losses
(three by KO)
Age at which title was won: 24 (20th fight)

JOE Frazier became champion in Muhammad Ali's enforced absence, but those who disputed his right to the title were silenced when he beat Ali on points in a brilliant and brutal battle in New York in 1971.

Like so many fighters before him, Frazier had used the boxing ring to escape the poverty trap. He was the seventh son in a family of 13 and worked on his father's run-down vegetable plantation from the age of seven. He followed his elder brothers to Philadelphia and got himself a job in what was, perhaps fittingly, a slaughterhouse.

Joe won 38 of his 40 amateur contests, his two defeats both being at the massive hands of Grand Rapids giant Buster Mathis. The second setback came in the US Olympic trials, but the victory cost the luckless Mathis a broken thumb and it was Frazier who went to Tokyo in his place and won the Olympic gold medal.

He fought like a black Rocky Marciano with a perpetual motion two-fisted style that earned him the nickname Smokin' Joe. In his first 28 months as a professional he hurried through 19 straight victories and then in 1968 he was matched with his old rival Mathis in a bout that was billed for the heavyweight title vacated by Ali. Frazier gave Mathis quite a mauling before the referee stopped the fight in the 11th round.

Frazier eventually beat Jimmy Ellis for the undisputed championship and then after outpointing comeback man Ali he had easy-pickings fights against Terry Daniels and Ron Stander before running into the formidable fists of George Foreman. Frazier was never the same force after his two-round demolition by Foreman.

He lost two storming fights with Ali and then in 1976 tried again to get the better of Foreman but was hammered to defeat in five rounds. At his peak, Smokin' Joe was one of the great champions, but his style of fighting left him too exposed to punches and he was tailor-made for a big hitter like Foreman.

 I believe in doing a job of work, not talking about it. Ali can do enough talking for both of us.

GEORGE FOREMAN 1973–1974; 1994
Born: Marshall, Texas, 10 January 1948
Height: 6ft 4in
Weight: 15st (210lb); 17st (238lb)
Reach: 82in
Chest: 42–44.5in
Fist: 12in
Nickname: The Punchin' Preacher
Career span: 1969–1977; 1987–1997
Record: 81 fights, 76 wins (68 KOs), five losses
(one by KO)
Age at which title was won: 25 (38th fight) and 45
(77th fight)

WHETHER the reign of George I or George II is taken into consideration, the astonishing George Foreman has assured himself of a lasting place in the boxing hall of fame. He stirred up the world punchbowl with his 'second coming' after a ten-year retirement, and at the age of 45 he took over from Jersey Joe Walcott as the oldest champion in heavyweight history when he blasted southpaw Michael Moorer to a tenth-round knockout defeat in Las Vegas on 5 November 1994.

Foreman had achieved enough the first time around to earn himself a rating in the 'great' category. Boxing followers were first alerted to his power when he won the gold medal in the 1968 Olympics. The fifth of seven children of a railroad construction worker, he used the boxing ring to save himself from a life of crime. George later had 12 children: five sons and seven daughters. All the boys were called George 'to make them feel equal'.

There was an almost novice-like rawness about his style that persuaded world champion Joe Frazier that he could handle him in what was intended as a warm-up fight for a rematch with Muhammad Ali. They met in Kingston, Jamaica, on 22 January 1973, Foreman's 25th birthday. Frazier was parted from his championship and a promised fortune in two rounds of unbridled savagery.

Foreman put his title on the line against Ali in the 'Rumble in the Jungle' in Zaire on 30 October 1974. Ali psyched him out of the fight and his championship. The eighth-round knockout defeat ended Foreman's unbeaten run of 40 fights.

For ten years Foreman pounded the Bible and set up a charity to help wayward youngsters in Texas. Then, shortly before his 40th birthday, he stunned the boxing world again by announcing his comeback. He was around 30lb heavier than in his championship days, and his shaven head gave him a menacing appearance totally alien to the image he had fashioned outside the ring as a preacher.

He gave Evander Holyfield all the trouble he could handle before going down to a 12-round points defeat in a title challenge in 1991.

Ol' George was rewarded for his persistence when he grabbed the WBA and IBF titles from Moorer. He made even more money than he had in the ring with his best-selling George Foreman Grill.

 I always invited God into my corner, but I had to do the fighting. Now I am in his corner fighting for his word to be heard.

LARRY HOLMES 1978–1985
Born: Cuthbert, Georgia, 3 November 1949
Height: 6ft 4in
Weight: 15st 3lb (213lb)
Reach: 81in
Chest: 45–48in
Fist: 13.5in
Nicknames: Black Cloud and Easton Assassin
Career span: 1973–1988; 1991–2002
Record: 75 fights, 69 wins (44 KOs), six defeats
Age at which title was won: 28 (28th fight)

LARRY Holmes found himself haunted by a living legend, Muhammad Ali, and a dead hero, Rocky Marciano, during a three-tier career in which he made a not-quite-accepted bid to be recognised as one of the greatest of all heavyweight champions. Like George Foreman, he decided to make a comeback as a 40-something fighting grandfather out to prove that the modern young contenders were just pretenders. He was convinced they were not in the same class as he had been when he ruled the world heavyweights for seven years while a fleet of Alphabet Boys sank out of sight like torpedoed ships in the night.

His comeback started in 1991, and by the spring of 1995 he had manoeuvred himself into a title fight against Oliver McCall. Holmes had first ascended to the WBC heavyweight throne on 10 June 1978, by narrowly outpointing Ken Norton in a classic 15 rounds contest.

During this early phase of his career Holmes was never able to exorcise the ghost of his phenomenally popular predecessor Muhammad Ali, whose performances and personality continually cast a giant shadow over just about every move that Holmes made. Even Holmes idolised Ali, for whom he used to work as a young sparring partner. It was one of the saddest days of his life when he forced Ali – dangerously weakened by shedding too much weight too quickly – to retire at the end of ten rounds in a title fight at Las Vegas in 1980.

The only way Holmes might have closed the gap on Ali in the never-ending 'Who's the greatest?' debate was to equal or beat Rocky Marciano's record of 49 unbeaten fights. He was one away from drawing level when he dropped a bitterly disputed points decision to light-heavyweight champion Michael Spinks in Las Vegas on 21 September 1985, and then lost the return match seven months later.

In 1987 he staged the first of two comebacks when, aged 38, he challenged for Mike Tyson's world crown. Even his $5m purse seemed small consolation for the humiliation and pain he suffered at the hands of a peak-power Tyson, who knocked him out in four rounds.

> Have you noticed that Foreman never calls me out or ever mentions my name? He is afraid of me like most fighters are, and most people want to forget about Larry Holmes, like he never ever existed.

MIKE TYSON 1986–1990; 1996
Born: Brooklyn, New York, 30 November 1966
Height: 5ft 10in
Weight: 16st (224lb)
Reach: 71in
Chest: 43–45in
Fist: 13in
Nicknames: Iron Mike and Mighty Mike
Career span: 1985–2005
Record: 58 fights, 50 wins (44 KOs), six losses (five by KO), two no contests
Age at which title was first won: 20 (28th fight)

MIKE Tyson became the world's youngest world heavyweight champion at 20 years four months and 22 days when he bombed out Trevor Berbick in two rounds on 22 November 1986. He emerged as the lineal champion in 1988, knocking out Michael Spinks in 91 seconds, and successfully defended his titles nine times. It was a trail of destruction that had fight fans comparing him with the greatest of all time.

But 'Typhoon Tyson' appeared to be cracking under the well-chronicled pressure of a broken marriage and a reported suicide attempt. Yet the boxing world was still astonished when he lost his title to a tenth-round knockout by James 'Buster' Douglas in Tokyo on 11 February 1990, in what was expected to be a routine defence.

There were complaints from the Tyson camp over a slow count that allowed Douglas to escape a possible knockout in the eighth round.

Tyson licked his wounds and was back in dynamic action four months later, winning in one round against Henry Tillman. On 8 December 1990 he knocked out Alex Stewart in one round in Atlantic City. Then in 1991 he had two wars with Razor Ruddock in Las Vegas, winning both of them, but with performances that made critics wonder if his best was behind him.

Following a three-year jail sentence for rape, he started his comeback in 1995 and was back as a champion when he comfortably relieved Frank Bruno of his WBC crown. With his defeat of Bruno, Tyson joined Floyd Patterson, Muhammad Ali, Tim Witherspoon, Evander Holyfield and George Foreman as the only men in boxing history to have regained the heavyweight championship.

He lost the WBA title to Evander Holyfield by an 11th-round stoppage, and in the return he was sensationally disqualified for biting Holyfield's ear.

In 2002, Tyson fought for the world heavyweight title again at the age of 35, losing by knockout to Lennox Lewis. He declared bankruptcy in 2003, despite having received an estimated $50m. Mike now enthrals audiences with tales of his incredible adventure that includes beating alcoholism, three marriages and his embrace of the Muslim religion. It's been quite a journey.

 I try to catch them right on the tip of the nose, because I try to punch the bone into the brain.

JAMES 'BUSTER' DOUGLAS 1990
Born: Columbus, Ohio, 7 April 1960
Height: 6ft 4in
Weight: 16st 8lb (232lb)
Reach: 84in
Chest: 44–48in
Fist: 13.5in
Career span: 1981–1990
Record: 46 fights, 38 wins (25 KOs), six losses (one by KO), one draw, one no contest
Age at which title was won: 29 (36th fight)

JAMES 'Buster' Douglas had two universally recognised world title fights during which he managed to cause first the biggest shock and then one of the biggest stinks in boxing history. His knockout defeat of Mike Tyson in 1990 was a performance of a lifetime in which he fought like a lion. Eight months later he went out like a lamb. He surrendered the crown so tamely to Evander Holyfield that it was almost impossible to believe that this was the same fighter who had vanquished the 'unbeatable' Tyson.

Douglas was taught to box by his father Billy Douglas, who had been a highly rated middleweight. Billy had the last fight of his long career only ten months before his son turned professional. Nicknamed 'Buster', James preferred basketball to boxing and won a two-year scholarship to a college in Kansas where his 6ft 4in height and his 84in reach made him a formidable force on the basketball court. It was after winning a junior Olympics boxing title that he decided to follow in his father's footsteps, but the way his weight see-sawed suggested he was not totally dedicated to his chosen profession.

Despite his great bulk, he rarely looked a big puncher and had stopped only 18 of his opponents. He fought Tony

Tucker for the paper IBF crown on 30 May 1987, and suddenly ran out of steam and ambition on his way to a painful tenth-round defeat.

It was one of six losses in a 35-fight career before he stepped into the Tokyo Dome ring on Sunday, 11 February 1990 for what everybody thought would be a ritual slaughter. But Tyson made the mistake of completely underestimating his challenger and paid the price with a tenth-round knockout defeat.

Buster seemed to be lacking condition and enthusiasm when he defended the title against Evander Holyfield eight months later and went down and out in the third round to the first heavy blow of the fight. In 1995 he started trying to shed weight from a massive 400lb bulk for a comeback and a hoped-for return with Tyson. He managed to get into reasonable shape but had none of the snap and sparkle of that night in Tokyo when he put out Tyson's lights. He later earned well from featuring in a popular computer game and acted in several films.

> My mother, who died three weeks before the fight with Tyson, was in the ring with me. She always told me, "You can do whatever you put your mind to." I put my mind to beating Tyson despite everybody writing me off.

EVANDER HOLYFIELD 1990–1992; 1993–1994; 1996–1999; 2000–2001

Born: Atmore, Alabama, 19 October 1962
Height: 6ft 2in
Weight: 15st 2lb (212lb)
Reach: 77in
Chest: 43–46in
Fist: 13in
Nickname: The Real Deal
Career span: 1984–2011
Record: 57 fights, 44 wins (29 KOs), ten losses, two draws, one no contest
Age at which title was first won: 28 (25th fight)

EVANDER Holyfield, 'The Real Deal', won his fights with style and precision in contrast to Mike Tyson's bludgeoning ferocity. Uniquely, he reigned as the undisputed champion in both the cruiserweight and heavyweight divisions. He is the only four-time world heavyweight champion, having held the WBA, WBC, IBF, and lineal titles from 1990 to 1992; the WBA, IBF, and lineal titles again from 1993 to 1994; the WBA title from 1996 to 1999; the IBF title from 1997 to 1999; and the WBA title for a fourth time from 2000 to 2001.

He launched his paid career as a cruiserweight after a disqualification cost him almost certain gold medal success in the 1984 Olympics. In only his 12th contest, in Atlanta on 12 July 1986, he took the world WBA title from Dwight Muhammad Qawi and defended it four times before pumping pounds on to his frame with a special diet and fitness programme (many years later he was accused of using steroids and human growth hormone to increase his bulk).

Holyfield made his debut in the heavyweight ranks as a solid 210lb force in 1988 with a fifth-round victory over James 'Quick' Tillis, and in 1990 took the title from Tyson's conqueror 'Buster' Douglas with an easy third-round knockout victory. The new champion outpointed the old champ George Foreman, and then had a laboured points victory over Larry Holmes. Five months later he lost a points verdict and his titles to Riddick Bowe. This was when Holyfield showed his great character, outpointing Bowe in a return fight interrupted by a parachuting skydiver invading the ring.

After losing to Michael Moorer in a brawling battle on 22 April 1994, Holyfield was diagnosed as having a heart condition. His comeback campaign included an eighth-round stoppage defeat in a thrilling rubber match with Riddick Bowe and back-to-back wars with Tyson and Lennox Lewis.

The father of 11 children by six different women, Holyfield hit financial problems despite earning more than $350m during his career.

Facing new allegations of using human growth hormone, he continued fighting right up until 2011. A born-again Christian, he gained new popularity on televised celebrity dance shows.

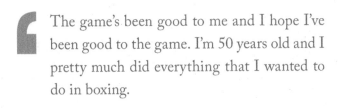

The game's been good to me and I hope I've been good to the game. I'm 50 years old and I pretty much did everything that I wanted to do in boxing.

RIDDICK BOWE 1992–1993
Born: Brooklyn, New York, 10 August 1967
Height: 6ft 5in
Weight: 17st 6lb (244lb)
Reach: 81in
Chest: 46–50in
Fist: 13in
Nickname: Big Daddy
Career span: 1989–1996; 2004–2008
Record: 45 fights, 43 wins (33 KOs), one loss, one no contest
Age at which title was won: 25 (31st fight)

RIDDICK 'Big Daddy' Bowe was briefly undisputed champion of the world until tossing the WBC belt into a dustbin rather than defend it against his old foe Lennox Lewis. Like Mike Tyson, Bowe was born and brought up in Brooklyn and used boxing as his springboard out of the ghetto. Lewis had raised doubts about his ability to absorb a punch when he stopped him in two rounds in the 1988 Olympic super-heavyweight final, but there was no sign of weakness under pressure throughout his professional career.

His peak performance came when he challenged Evander Holyfield for the three main titles at Las Vegas on 13 November 1992, surviving an early crisis to to win an epic battle on points. He defended the WBA and IBF belts against Michael Dokes and Jesse Ferguson before losing them back to Holyfield in another war in Las Vegas on 6 November 1993. This points loss was his only defeat as a professional.

He was back as a champion in March 1995 when he knocked out Herbie Hide in six rounds to win the WBO title, becoming the first boxer in history to win the championships of all four major sanctioning bodies –

the WBA, WBC, IBF, and WBO. Later that year, Bowe vacated the WBO title in order to fight Holyfield for a third time, and won dramatically in the eighth round, the first opponent to stop Evander.

Bowe retired after two back-to-back wars with Andrew Golota, with the rugged Pole disqualified in both fights. After being found guilty of domestic violence against his wife, he served a prison sentence and then made a low-key return to the ring in 2004, retiring a second time after notching three more victories. He tried wrestling, kickboxing, briefly joined the Marines and was always restless.

A man of wild mood swings, he made great humanitarian gestures by pledging huge donations to international charities. He was worth $15m, and spent it on ten houses and 26 cars. The millennium, however, brought bankruptcy, with an expensive divorce. He touched rock bottom in 2017 when starting a crowdfunding appeal to save his last remaining house from being repossessed.

 I hope people are willing to help me after all the entertainment the old champ gave them in the ring. Things have not been so good lately.

LENNOX LEWIS 1992–1994; 1999–2004
Born: Stratford, London, 2 September 1965
Height: 6ft 5in
Weight: 17st (238lb)
Reach: 84in
Chest: 46–48in
Fist: 14in
Nickname: The Lion
Career span: 1989–2003
Record: 44 fights, 41 wins (32 KOs), two losses (two by KO), one draw
Age at which title was won: 27 (23rd fight)

LENNOX Lewis became the first British-born world heavyweight champion since Bob Fitzsimmons when he was awarded the WBC belt after Riddick Bowe had relinquished it by throwing it in a dustbin. Lewis was rated champion on account of his sensational two-round stoppage of Razor Ruddock in a final eliminator at Earls Court on 31 October 1992.

Standing 6ft 5in and weighing 17st, Lewis launched his professional career under the management of Frank (now Kellie) Maloney in London. He had first come to prominence when stopping Riddick Bowe in two rounds to win the Olympic super-heavyweight gold medal for his adopted country of Canada in the 1988 Seoul Games.

In Britain, he was continually being compared to Frank Bruno and the two great rivals met in a bitter showdown in Cardiff on 1 October 1993. Bruno was giving a good account of himself until walking into a left hook in the seventh round. He was forced back on to the ropes, and the referee had to rescue him.

Lewis, later trained by master motivator Emanuel Steward, defended the title three times before an upset knockout defeat by Oliver McCall at Wembley Arena in 1994. Lewis avenged the loss in a 1997 rematch to win back the WBC championship.

In 1998 Lewis won the lineal title by defeating Shannon Briggs. Two fights against Evander Holyfield in 1999 (the first of which ended in a controversial draw) saw Lewis become undisputed heavyweight champion by unifying his WBC title with Holyfield's WBA and IBF belts, as well as the vacant IBO crown.

Lewis, a poker player and chess expert, was knocked out by Hasim Rahman in a 2001 upset, but this defeat was avenged later in the year. In 2002, he stopped Mike Tyson in eight rounds.

In what would be his final fight Lewis defeated Vitali Klitschko in six bloody rounds in June 2003. He announced his retirement in 2004, and has turned down all inducements to come back, preferring to spend his time with his wife, former beauty queen Violet Chang, and their four children in luxury homes in Florida and Jamaica. He has funded an after-school chess programme for disadvantaged youths, one of whom earned a university chess scholarship at Tennessee Tech.

> In boxing you create a strategy to beat each new opponent. It's just like my favourite pastime of chess.

SHANNON BRIGGS 1997–1998; 2006–2007
Born: Brooklyn, New York, 4 December 1971
Height: 6ft 4in
Weight: 18st (252lb)
Reach: 80in
Chest: 46–48in
Fist: 14in
Nickname: The Cannon
Career span: 1989–1996; 2004–2008
Record: 67 fights, 60 wins (53 KOs), six defeats (two by KO), one draw
Age at which title was won: 25 (31st fight)

IN a three-part, 20-year career, Shannon Briggs was a two-time world heavyweight champion, holding the coveted lineal title from 1997 to 1998, and the WBO championship from 2006 to 2007. Nicknamed Shannon the Cannon, he became 'the man who beat the man' when scoring a shock majority points decision over once-mighty George Foreman at the Trump Taj Majal Hotel and Casino in Atlantic City.

After capturing the WBA and IBF titles from Michael Moorer in 1994, Foreman forfeited both but retained the lineal championship, which then passed on to Briggs after his shock victory. Big George picked up a $5m purse, while Briggs was paid just $400,000.

Three months later Briggs put his lineal title on the line against Lennox Lewis and was flattened in five rounds. Lewis collected $4m and the Briggs purse was $1m.

Briggs went back to fighting low-ranked fighters for the next seven years, and after 17 wins and two losses won the WBO heavyweight title in 2006 when he knocked out Sergei Liakhovich in the last round while trailing on points. Proof that he was a power puncher is that 34 of his opponents did not hear the bell for the second round, but he lacked staying power and struggled when fights went past the halfway mark. He had a huge hulk to shift around the ring. Briggs challenged Vitali Klitschko for the WBC crown in Hamburg in 2010, and was in intensive care in hospital after losing heavily on points over 12 brutal rounds.

Trying his luck at kickboxing, Briggs knocked out Tom Erikson, a mixed martial artist with a background in collegiate wrestling, just over a minute into round one in Saitama, Japan, on 27 March 2004.

An asthmatic who spent several of his school-age years homeless and living on the streets, Briggs was suspended by the WBA in 2017 after failing a drug test. At one stage his weight ballooned up to 400lb and he admitted he had considered suicide, another low point in his roller-coaster life. Post-boxing, he developed a successful career as a film actor. What an incredible character.

‘ When I was a kid, me and my mother were in a tough situation where we lost our home. We got out of it through the help of friends and really through boxing. It was boxing that got me off the streets and got me to where I could make money and have a place to live.

VITALI KLITSCHKO 1999–2000; 2004–2005; 2008–2013

Born: Belovodskoye, Kirghiz SSR (now Kyrgyzstan), 19 July 1971
Height: 6ft 7in
Weight: 17st 7lb (245lb)
Reach: 79in
Chest: 45–47in
Fist: 13in
Nickname: Dr Ironfist
Career span: 1996–2012
Record: 47 fights, 45 wins (32 KOs), two losses
Age at which title was won: 27 (23rd fight)

VITALI Klitschko, extraordinary boxer turned politician, is a three-time world champion, the second-longest reigning WBC heavyweight champion, has the third-longest combined world championship reign at 2,735 days, made nine consecutive defences and had the fourth-longest combined title streak in modern boxing at 15 bouts.

He held the WBO title from 1999 to 2000; the *Ring* magazine championship from 2004 to 2005; and the WBC belt twice, from 2004 to 2005 and from 2008 to 2013.

Nicknamed 'Dr Ironfist' because of his PhD degree, he stood 6ft 7in and dominated the ring with well-thought-out strategy and long-range power hitting. With an 87.23 per cent knockout ratio, he holds one of the highest figures of any world champion, and he was blessed with a strong chin. His two losses in 47 fights came because of a shoulder injury (against Chris Byrd) and a deep cut above his eye (against Lennox Lewis in the sixth round of a world title unification showdown).

Vitali is the only heavyweight boxer to receive the WBC honour of 'Eternal Champion' after successfully defending the title ten times. He is also the only world heavyweight champion never to have taken a count, and he and George Foreman are the only heavyweight boxers in history to defend a world title after turning 40. His brother Wladimir, five years younger having been born on 25 March 1976, is a 6ft 6in Ukrainian who won 64 of 69 fights from 1996 until his retirement in 2017 after an 11th-round stoppage by Anthony Joshua, which came 18 months after his previous bout, a points defeat to Tyson Fury. A two-time world heavyweight champion, he held the WBA (Super), IBF and WBO crowns, as well as the IBO, *Ring* magazine, and lineal titles. Wladmir has the second-most total successful title defences of any heavyweight boxer with 23. He fought in a record 29 heavyweight title fights, and holds the record of beating the most boxers with an undefeated career (12), and also defeated ten current or former world champions.

Wladimir speaks four languages, is a professor who gives university lectures, and has poured money into youth projects in Kyiv.

The Klitschkos dominated world and European heavyweight boxing from 2006 to 2015. Vitali became an MP and then mayor of Kyiv, and both brothers have been prominent as motivators in the bloody Ukrainian war with the invading Russians.

 I have been a fighter all my life and will fight for Ukraine to my last breath. My brother Wladimir and I are now interested in only one victory and that is beating Putin and his invading army.

HASIM RAHMAN 2001; 2005–2006

Born: Baltimore, Maryland, 7 November 1972
Height: 6ft 2in
Weight: 17st (238lb)
Reach: 82in
Chest: 46–48in
Fist: 14in
Nickname: The Rock
Career span: 1994–2014
Record: 62 fights, 50 wins (41 KOs), nine losses (six by KO), two draws, one no contest
Age at which title was won: 28 (37th fight)

HASIM Rahman rocked Lennox Lewis and shocked the boxing world with a punch-out-of-the-blue that caused one of the greatest ever ring upsets. The punch – a Marciano-style overarm right – landed flush on the jaw of Lewis and knocked him cold in round five of what was expected to be a routine title defence in Brakpan, South Africa, on 22 April 2001.

Lewis had to go to court to get Rahman to honour a return-fight clause after great dictator Don King stepped in as the champion's new manager and tried to get him an easier first defence. Showing the character that marked his career, Lewis won the rematch with a convincing fourth-round revenge knockout in Las Vegas on 17 November 2001.

Boxing had saved Rahman from a life of crime, and before becoming disciplined to a training and fighting regime he had been involved in the drugs scene in the back streets of Baltimore. It was a points victory over former world champion Trevor Berbick in his 18th fight, in Atlantic City, that flagged him as a hot prospect.

Rahman made three comebacks during his eventful 20-year career, and reached a new peak in 2005 when he won the WBC title (initially the interim version) for a second time by defeating Monte Barrett.

He was elevated to full champion status by the year's end following the retirement of Vitali Klitschko, but lost it 12 months later when old rival Oleg Maskaev stopped him in the 12th and last round.

In December 2008 his latest comeback bid came to a shuddering halt when he fought Wladimir Klitschko as a late replacement for injured David Haye. The referee stopped a one-sided slaughter in the seventh round.

After failing to take the WBA title from Alexander Povetkin in Hamburg in 2012, his have-gloves-will-travel policy took him down to New Zealand for a meaningless eight-man tournament in 2014. He was finally persuaded to hang up his gloves following a points defeat by club fighter Anthony Nansen.

Since retirement, Rahman has worked as a ringside summariser for televised boxing shows.

> When I was growing up in Baltimore I felt like I was in a maze with no exit. There were only two ways out, death or the penitentiary. Then I discovered boxing and it gave shape and meaning to my life.

TYSON FURY 2015–2016; 2020–
Born: Wythenshawe, Manchester, 12 August 1988
Height: 6ft 9in
Weight: 19st 7lb (273lb)
Reach: 85in
Chest: 48–50in
Fist: 15in
Nickname: The Gypsy King
Career span: 2008–
Record: 34 fights, 33 wins (24 KOs), one draw
Age at which title was won: 27 (25th fight)

THE eccentric and exceptional Tyson Fury brought earthquaking shocks to the world heavyweight division when he outpointed Wladimir Klitschko in the Ukrainian's adopted back yard of Dusseldorf in Germany on 28 November 2015. It meant that against all odds the 6ft 9in giant known as the Gypsy King had captured the unified WBA (Super), IBF, WBO, IBO, *Ring* magazine and lineal heavyweight titles. The totally unexpected victory (but predicted by Fury and his fanatical followers) earned him the Fighter of the Year and Upset of the Year awards from *Ring*.

Fury out-thought and out-fought the master strategist, often baffling the long-time champion by fighting with both hands behind his back and taunting him with punches thrown from unexpected angles. It was an extraordinary exhibition of unorthodox yet effective tactics.

This was Tyson at the top of the mountain, but he was suddenly back in the foothills as he fell out with the boxing establishment through a long-running series of spats. First he was stripped of the IBF title for preferring a money-making return with Klitschko to a defence against mandatory challenger Vyacheslav Glazkov. In 2016, Fury abdicated the WBA, WBO, IBO, and lineal thrones following a medical investigation and personal issues, and two cancellations of the Klitschko rematch. Following more than two years of inactivity, *Ring* stripped him of his last remaining title.

His problems were largely drug-related, and he fell out with the British Boxing Board of Control to the point where he was threatening to apply for an Irish boxing licence after tracing his ancestry to Belfast and Galway. As an amateur he had represented both England and Ireland, winning the ABA super-heavyweight title in 2008 before turning professional later that year.

He got himself involved in widespread controversy over homophobic remarks, and this larger-than-life character was still waiting to make his comeback to the ring as 2018 dawned by which time Anthony Joshua had stolen his thunder and his titles.

But while Joshua ran into difficulties, Fury – scaling down from 27st to 20st – went from strength to strength in a sensational comeback and became number one in the world again by overcoming the previously undefeated Deontay Wilder in a thrilling three-fight serial that revealed Fury not only as King of the Gypsies but King of the World.

He miraculously got off the canvas in the final round of their first fight to force a draw, and then clubbed Wilder to a seventh-round defeat in their second contest and stopped him in 11 brutal rounds in the third fight.

Fury's sing-alongs at the end of his title bouts have helped his fame transcend boxing, and he was hitting the right notes again in April 2022 when stopping Dillian Whyte in six rounds in front of a world record 94,000 crowd at Wembley.

In December 2022, Fury stopped old foe Derek Chisora in ten rounds and talked about a showdown with unbeaten Ukrainian Oleksandr Usyk.

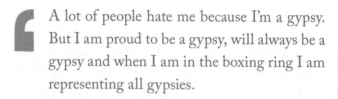

A lot of people hate me because I'm a gypsy. But I am proud to be a gypsy, will always be a gypsy and when I am in the boxing ring I am representing all gypsies.

ANTHONY JOSHUA 2016–2019; 2019–2021
Born: Watford, Hertfordshire, 15 October 1989
Height: 6ft 6in
Weight: 17st 12lb (250lb)
Reach: 82in
Chest: 48–50in
Fist: 14in
Nickname: AJ
Career span: 2013–
Record: 27 fights, 24 wins (22 KOs), three losses
(one by KO)
Age at which title was won: 27 (16th fight, IBF belt)

WINNER of the Olympic gold medal in the 2012 London Olympics, AJ came of age when he got off the canvas to hammer Wladimir Klitschko to an 11th-round defeat to add the WBA and IBO titles to his IBF crown in only his 19th professional fight. Then on 31 March 2018 the Watford giant took the WBO championship from New Zealander Joseph Parker in Cardiff.

Carefully promoted by the Eddie Hearn/Barry Hearn Matchroom stable and trained by Rob McCracken, Joshua made a rapid rise to the top of the heavyweight heap, and this personable young man proved he had turned his life right round from when he was an 18-year-old bricklayer with drug-world connections and problems with the law.

Watford-born to Nigerian parents, AJ did not start boxing until he was 18 and rapidly established himself as an outstanding amateur with Finchley ABC. With the Olympic title as his calling card, he turned professional in 2013 and quickly annexed the British and Commonwealth heavyweight crowns. His first world title followed in 2016 when he knocked out defending IBF champion Charles Martin in the second round at the O2 Arena.

Following his convincing 12-round points victory over the previously unbeaten Parker, Joshua was being lined up for a unification battle with undefeated American Deontay Wilder, who had been whipping up a storm with his performances.

The 6ft 7in Bronze Bomber from Tuscaloosa, Alabama – winner of a bronze medal in the 2008 Olympics – collected the WBC heavyweight title on the way to 40 successive victories, all but one inside the distance. Between them he and Joshua breathed new life into a heavyweight division that seemed out on its feet. Then along came Tyson Fury and knocked the breath out of Wilder.

Everybody was looking forward to an AJ–Tyson Fury showdown when Joshua was stopped in seven rounds in a shock defeat by Mexican Andy Ruiz Jr. in New York in the summer of 2019. AJ won the title back with a convincing points victory six months later in Saudi Arabia.

Again with the drums beating for Joshua v Fury, AJ was twice outpointed in back-to-back world title battles with brilliant Ukrainian Oleksandr Usyk, first at the Tottenham Football Stadium and then in Saudi Arabia.

> I owe everything to the sport of boxing. I was a wild young man on the way to nowhere when I was saved by the disciplines and challenges of the ring. Boxing has equipped me for life and has taught me how to behave with control and respect in and out of the ring.

ANDY RUIZ JR. 2019
Born: Imperial, California, 11 September 1989
Height: 6ft 2in
Weight: 18st 13lb (265lb)
Reach: 74in
Chest: 44–47in
Fist: 14in
Nickname: Destroyer
Career span: 2009–
Record: 37 fights, 35 wins (22 KOs), two defeats
(one by KO)
Age at which title was won: 29 (34th fight)

Ruiz created a shock that could have been measured on the Richter scale when he stopped British idol Anthony Joshua in New York in June 2019 to become the first fighter of Mexican heritage – although born in California, his parents are Mexican – to win the world heavyweight crown.

His reign lasted just six months before Joshua regained the title with a unanimous points victory in Saudi Arabia, with Ruiz blaming his defeat on having partied too much since winning the championship.

Bilingual, he had represented Mexico in the 2008 Beijing Olympics before turning professional after a long amateur career in which he lost just five of 105 contests.

His grandfather owned a gymnasium in Mexico and this is where he learned his craft. He developed into an accomplished box-fighter with fast combination punches and famed for a granite jaw and a huge heart.

He was a 25/1 underdog against the then unbeaten Joshua when summoned as a substitute opponent for Jarrell Miller, who failed a drugs test. It was supposed to be a showcase fight for AJ in his American debut, but he totally underestimated Californian-based Ruiz, who got off the canvas in the third round to overpower the heavily muscled Brit. The referee stopped the fight in the seventh with Joshua under heavy fire and looking confused and bemused.

Six months later, AJ got his act together and comfortably outpointed Ruiz, who could find none of the fire he had shown in their first fight.

Now fabulously rich, Ruiz continued his career in 2020 but without the hungry fighter motivation. He joked that he had to keep fighting to feed his wife and four children, but the two fights with Joshua had moved him into the wealthy zone.

> I partied non-stop for three months after taking the title from Joshua, and was not in proper condition either physically or psychologically for the return fight, otherwise I would still be champion.

OLEKSANDR USYK 2021–

Born: Simferopol, Ukraine, 17 January 1987
Height: 6ft 3in
Weight: 13st to 15st
Reach: 78in
Chest: 46in
Fist: 13.5in
Nickname: The Cat
Career span: 2013–
Record: 20 fights, 20 wins (13 KOs)
Age at which title was won: 34 (19th fight; third at heavyweight)

THE Olympic heavyweight champion in London in 2012, Usyk quickly made an impact in the professional ranks and was undefeated world cruiserweight champion from his tenth fight in 2018 before stepping up to heavyweight. He is considered one of the most accomplished boxers ever to come from eastern Europe, where he was a renowned amateur after losing just 15 of 335 contests.

In defences of his cruiserweight title he beat five former or current world champions. Despite being outweighed and outreached, Usyk gave two brilliant boxing exhibitions to take Anthony Joshua's heavyweight crown in September 2021 and then master him in the return a year later. At 37, he was hailed as the best active pound-for-pound fighter in the world.

Starting his professional career under the guidance of the Klitschko brothers, Usyk quickly established himself as one of the most formidable fighters in the world. His strengths were the boxing skill and punching speed of a middleweight combined with the heart of a lion and the punching power of a heavyweight.

Once he had proved himself unbeatable in the cruiserweight division, he set his sights on the heavyweight crown, despite having to concede height and weight to the real giants of the ring. Many thought he was reaching too high when he challenged Joshua. But he outboxed the Brit in their first fight and mastered him again in a second contest staged in Saudi Arabia. He was not only proving himself an exceptional champion but was becoming exceedingly wealthy.

The drums started beating for a titles-unifying showdown between Usyk and Tyson Fury, with the Ukrainian insisting he was not concerned about the Gypsy King having considerable reach and weight advantage. He was fearless.

Married to a Russian and a fluent speaker of the language, Usyk proudly insists that he is 'Ukrainian through and through' and volunteered to join the defence of his nation when the Russian invasion started in 2022. Early in his professional career he was guided by the Klitschko brothers, and joined them in condemnation of President Putin's war against Ukraine.

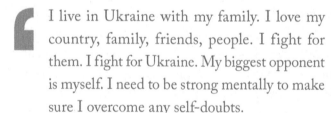

I live in Ukraine with my family. I love my country, family, friends, people. I fight for them. I fight for Ukraine. My biggest opponent is myself. I need to be strong mentally to make sure I overcome any self-doubts.

The Alphabet Boys

THE WORLD heavyweight scene has become clouded in confusion by the proliferation of so-called world governing bodies recognising a queue of different title-holders. There was the World Boxing Association (WBA), the World Boxing Council (WBC), the International Boxing Federation (IBF) and, later, the World Boxing Organisation (WBO), all of whom were dishing out championships to a parade of boxers who have become known as the Alphabet Boys. There have also been others trying to make an initial impact, for instance the IBO, WBF, IBC and WBU. It is all in danger of diluting the value of what has always been considered the number one prize in sport.

This, in processional order, is how the main 'Alphabet Boys' won and lost their crowns.

ERNIE TERRELL, WBA 1965–1967

Ernie Terrell, born 4 April 1939, was the first of the pretenders to the heavyweight throne. The WBA stripped Muhammad Ali of his championship because he entered into a return-match agreement with Sonny Liston. Terrell, a 6ft 6in giant from Chicago via Mississippi, was nominated to fight veteran Eddie Machen and outpointed him on 5 March 1965. He won on points against George Chuvalo and Doug Jones in title defences before a summit showdown with Ali in Houston on 6 February 1967.

Ali handed out a humiliating hiding over 15 rounds, during which he repeatedly demanded that Terrell should call him by his new name instead of Cassius Clay. Terrell, the human skyscraper, was never the same force after his hammering by Ali. He died in Illinois on 16 December 1914 aged 75, suffering from dementia.

JIMMY ELLIS, WBA 1968–1970

Jimmy Ellis, born 24 February 1940, came from the same Louisville background as Muhammad Ali, and was one of Ali's best friends as well as his chief sparring partner. He outpointed Jerry Quarry on 27 April 1968, to win the WBA version of the title after Ali had been forced to surrender the crown because of his refusal to join the army.

Ellis successfully defended the title with a controversial points win against Floyd Patterson in Sweden on 14 September 1968, before being matched with Joe Frazier for the undisputed championship in New York on 16 February 1970. Smokin' Joe floored Ellis at the end of the fourth round with a devastating left hook. He was saved by the bell, but was in no condition to come out for the fifth round.

A stylish, upright boxer, Ellis continued to tour as a sparring partner with Ali, but dropped out of championship contention because of eye problems. He died in 2014, suffering from dementia.

KEN NORTON, WBC 1978

Ken Norton, born Jacksonville, Illinois, on 9 August 1945, was a 'paper' champion, the title being handed to him by the WBC after Leon Spinks had refused to defend against him because of his return match with Ali.

Norton was named champion on account of a title eliminator victory over Jimmy Young in Las Vegas on 25 November 1977, but he more than any of the other Alphabet Boys deserves his places in this trip through the history of the world heavyweight champions because of his three marvellous battles with Ali. He broke Ali's jaw and outpointed him in their first contest in San Diego on 31 March 1973, and many spectators considered him unlucky to be judged a points loser in their two other meetings on 10 September 1973 and 28 September 1976.

Norton had a magnificent physique and good boxing skills, but his reign was brief. Larry Holmes edged him out in a tremendous battle in Las Vegas on 9 June 1978.

His promising Hollywood acting career was finished by a car crash that left him partly crippled. His son, also Ken, was a heralded American football star and has created history by being on the winning side in three successive Super Bowls.

Norton died in 2013 following a series of strokes.

JOHN TATE, WBA 1979–1980

John Tate, born Marion City, Arkansas, on 29 January 1955, became one of the biggest of all heavyweight champions when he outpointed South African Gerrie Coetzee for the vacant WBA title in Pretoria on 20 October 1979. Standing 6ft 4in and weighing 17st 2lb (240lb), he captured the championship in his 20th contest. He lost the title in dramatic fashion in his first defence on 31 March 1980, when Mike Weaver produced an explosive punch to knock his man-mountain opponent down and out in the last minute of their 15-round battle.

Tate had turned professional after being hammered to a first-round defeat by Teofilo Stevenson in the 1976 Olympic semi-finals. Following his knockout by Weaver, his hopes of getting back into the title reckoning were shattered when Trevor Berbick beat him in nine rounds in Montreal on 20 June 1980.

His career was then wrecked by an addiction to drugs and alcohol, and he was given a three-year prison term for breaking a man's jaw while robbing him of $14. He was killed in a car crash in 1998, aged 43.

MIKE WEAVER, WBA 1980–1982

Mike Weaver, born Gatesville, Texas, on 14 June 1952, was always a dangerous opponent provided he could get past the first round. A mighty muscled black Adonis of a fighter, he had a string of first-round knockout defeats in a see-sawing career. His greatest moments were knocking out John Tate in the final minute to win the WBA title in Knoxville on 31 March 1980, and then defending it with a knock out win over Gerrie Coetzee in Bophuthatswana on 25 October 1980, and a points victory over James 'Quick' Tillis on 3 October 1981.

His world came apart when Mike Dokes stopped him in 63 seconds of his third defence in Las Vegas on 10 December 1982. Weaver, nicknamed Hercules, claimed he could have continued and screamed for a return. He came within a whisker of regaining the title, drawing with Dokes over 15 gruelling rounds.

His career continued late into his 30s, but he was never able to recapture the form of his peak years. His long career ended at the age of 49 with a sixth-round stoppage by Larry Holmes in 2000.

MIKE DOKES, WBA 1982–1983

Mike Dokes, born Akron, Ohio, on 10 August 1958, messed up what could have been one of the great careers in heavyweight boxing by getting involved in the drugs scene that is a black cloud over the American fight game. He was undefeated when he grabbed the WBA version of the world title from Mike Weaver in 1982 with a sensational 63-second victory that caused an uproar of controversy. 'Dynamite' Dokes had rocked Weaver with a big left hook, but most spectators thought the referee was too hasty in stopping the fight.

Dokes clung on to the title by drawing with Weaver but then suffered the first defeat of his career when he was clubbed to a tenth-round defeat by Gerrie Coetzee at Richfield on 23 September 1983.

His arrest on a drugs charge suddenly wrecked his comeback campaign. After rehabilitation treatment, he returned to the ring, but stoppages by Razor Ruddock and Evander Holyfield, followed by a return to his drug habit, pushed him out of championship contention. Dokes died of liver cancer at a hospice in Akron in August 2012, a day after his 54th birthday.

GERRIE COETZEE, WBA 1983–1984

Gerrie Coetzee, born Boksburg, South Africa, on 4 August 1955, was known as the 'Bionic Man' because of revolutionary surgery on his feared right hand, which prolonged his career.

He was a devastating puncher, as he proved when stopping Leon Spinks in one round in Monte Carlo in 1979.

Because of the poisonous politics of his country, Coetzee found it difficult to get top contenders into the ring with him, but when he finally got his title chance in 1983 he proved too powerful for Mike Dokes, stopping him in the tenth round to become the first South African to win the world heavyweight crown.

He lost the WBA title in controversial circumstances, getting stopped by Greg Page in an eighth round that ran into overtime in Sun City on 1 December 1984. Coetzee's chances of getting back on to the title bandwagon ended with a shattering first-round knockout defeat by British heavyweight hope Frank Bruno at Wembley in 1986.

His attempted comeback was halted by a tenth-round knockout by Iran Barkley on 8 June 1977. A biopic on Coetzee was released in 2022, called *Against All Odds*.

TIM WITHERSPOON, WBC 1984; WBA 1985–1986

Tim Witherspoon, born in Philadelphia on 27 December 1957, was nicknamed 'Terrible Tim' by Muhammad Ali in the days when he hired the young Philadelphian as his sparring partner.

Witherspoon thought he had won the WBC title in his 16th professional fight but a disputed points decision went to Larry Holmes. When Holmes switched to the newly founded International Boxing Federation (IBF), Witherspoon outpointed Greg Page for the vacant WBC crown on 9 March 1984.

His reign was brief, Pinklon Thomas taking the title from him with a points win five months later. Witherspoon became only the third champion to regain the title when he outpointed Tony Tubbs in 1985, this time for the WBA version.

He beat a drugs habit and after a successful title defence against Frank Bruno at Wembley Stadium on 19 July 1986 he looked set for a big-money showdown with Mike Tyson. But then he was bombed to a stunning first-round defeat by James 'Bonecrusher' Smith in New York on 12 December 1986, after which he became frozen out of the title scene following a bitter legal battle with promoter Don King.

He kept fighting into the 1990s but could never force his way back into the title picture. Tim returned home to Philly and became an in-demand trainer following his retirement, including working with his lightweight fighter son, also Tim.

GREG PAGE, WBA 1984–1985

Greg Page, born on 25 October 1958, was out of the same Louisville, Kentucky, territory as Muhammad Ali and Jimmy Ellis. After a brilliant amateur career, he chalked up 23 successive wins as a professional to earn a fight with Tim Witherspoon for the vacant WBC title on 9 March 1984.

Witherspoon outpointed him, but within nine months Page had helped himself to a title by stopping Gerrie Coetzee in the eighth round of an eventful WBA championship contest in Sun City. A timekeeping error meant the round ran into extra time and it was in the closing moments that Page pounded Coetzee to defeat when by rights the South African should have been sitting on his stool.

But the musical chairs with the title continued when Page was outpointed by Tony Tubbs at Buffalo, New York, on 29 April 1985. Page never really lived up to his early potential and drifted out of the ratings.

On 9 March 2001 he suffered brain damage when knocked out by Dale Crowe at Erlanger in Kentucky, and he was disabled for the rest of his life, dying in 2009 aged 50. He received $1.2m in damages because there were no medical facilities at the venue where he had his disastrous last fight.

PINKLON THOMAS, WBC 1985–1986

Pinklon Thomas, born Pontiac, Michigan, on 10 February 1957, appeared to be the best of the new crop of 'dreadnought' heavyweights and realised his potential when outpointing Tim Witherspoon to win the WBC championship in Las Vegas on 31 August 1984.

He looked set for a long reign and an eighth-round knockout defeat of Mike Weaver on 15 June 1985 seemed to confirm that he was a class above most other contenders. It was one of the biggest shocks of the decade when he lost his unbeaten record and his title to Trevor Berbick at Las Vegas on 22 March 1986.

Pinklon started a comeback eight months later with a victory over William Hosea, but he went on the slide after taking a hammering from Mike Tyson in a world championship contest at Las Vegas on 30 May 1987.

Like so many of the other Alphabet Boys, he got mixed up with drugs but he managed to beat the habit, and then became a trial horse opponent for up-and-coming prospects with much less talent than he showed in the early stages of his career.

After retirement, Thomas launched a foundation, Project P.I.N.K. (Pride in Neighbourhood Kids), and became a motivational speaker.

TONY TUBBS, WBA 1985–1986

Tony Tubbs, born Cincinnati, Ohio, on 15 February 1959, was nicknamed 'TNT', but he was not an explosive puncher, relying on skill to emerge as a title challenger. Tubbs was surprisingly light on his feet and a slick boxer considering his enormous 230lb bulk. He won the WBA title by smartly outpointing Greg Page in what was tagged as 'The Buffalo Blockbuster' on 29 April 1985, but he was then outmauled by Tim Witherspoon in his first defence on 17 January 1986.

It was announced after the fight that Witherspoon had failed a drugs test and he was ordered to give Tubbs a return, but he took step-aside money so that Tim could defend against Frank Bruno – a fight that he won in the 11th round.

After being blasted to a second-round defeat by Mike Tyson in Tokyo on 21 March 1988, Tubbs admitted to being hooked on cocaine.

When he hit the comeback trail in 1991 he dropped a disputed points decision to the rising young prospect Riddick Bowe. In March 1992 he tested positive for cocaine in Las Vegas, and was ordered to do 100 hours of community service after being suspended by the Nevada Boxing Commission.

Tubbs, who fathered 16 children, was inducted into the California and Indiana Boxing Halls of Fame.

MICHAEL SPINKS, IBF 1985–1988

Michael Spinks, born in St Louis on 13 July 1956, was the 1976 Olympic middleweight gold medallist and after an unbeaten four-year reign as one of the greatest of all world light-heavyweight champions he challenged Larry Holmes for the IBF crown at Las Vegas on 21 September 1985.

Inspired by the wonderfully eccentric and dynamic manager-promoter Butch Lewis, he put on more than 20lb and the performance of a lifetime to outpoint the previously undefeated Holmes and to follow his brother, Leon, as heavyweight king.

Just to show it was no fluke, he outpointed Holmes in the return match. Both decisions were angrily disputed by Holmes.

An easy victory by Spinks over Norway's European champion Steffan Tangstadon on 6 September 1986 set him up for a championship showdown with Mike Tyson in Atlantic City on 27 June 1988. Spinks folded in just 91 seconds against 'Iron Mike', and cried all the way to the bank as he announced his retirement after this first defeat as a professional.

He later sued the estate of his late manager and best friend Lewis for alleged mismanagement of his finances. Elected to the Boxing Hall of Fame, he lived in luxury in Delaware and said, 'This is what I fought for, to have an easy later life.'

TREVOR BERBICK, WBC 1986

Trevor Berbick, born Port Anthony, Jamaica, on 1 August 1953, caused a major upset when he outpointed Pinklon Thomas to win the WBC belt in Las Vegas on 22 March 1986. It was his second bid for the title, having been outpointed by Larry Holmes five years earlier.

He was Muhammad Ali's last opponent and scored a ten-round points victory in 1981 that at last convinced the great old champ that he should hang up his gloves. It was Berbick who stood between Mike Tyson and history in Las Vegas on 22 November 1986. But he did not stand for long, getting knocked down and stopped in two explosive rounds as Tyson became the youngest champion of them all.

Berbick later ran into difficulties both inside and outside the ring. At one stage the man who used to be a preacher had charges ranging against him that included theft, mortgage fraud, rape and assault, and – like his old rival Tyson – he was sent to prison.

He resumed boxing on his release as Israel T. Berbick, and in his eighth comeback fight at the age of 40 was outpointed by Jimmy Thunder for the obscure Continental Americas title. In October 2006 Berbick was murdered by his 20-year-old nephew and an accomplice following a dispute over land rights.

JAMES SMITH, WBA 1986

James 'Bonecrusher' Smith, born Magnolia, North Carolina, on 3 April 1955, came in as a late substitute for the allegedly injured Tony Tubbs against Tim Witherspoon in New York on 12 December 1986, and snatched the WBA title away with a sensational smash-and-grab first-round victory.

Witherspoon, who held a points decision over Smith, was battered to the canvas three times and stopped on the three-knockdown rule. The victory made 'Bonecrusher' the 'Cinderella Man' of the 1980s. He had not started boxing until the age of 23 while serving as a sergeant in the US Army after graduating from college.

After coming from behind to hand Frank Bruno his first defeat at Wembley on 13 May 1984, he failed in a bid for the IBF title held by Larry Holmes, who stopped him in 12 rounds on 9 November 1984.

Smith was outpointed by Mike Tyson in an uninspiring fight for the undisputed title on 7 March 1987, and during a comeback campaign was beaten by Razor Ruddock and then, after a long sequence of victories, surprisingly dropped a points decision to Levi Billups on 4 November 1991.

Nicknamed 'Bonecrusher' by London promoter Mike Barrett ('Jim Smith sounded fairly tame'), Smith became an ordained minister in 1996 and dedicated his life to youth-motivational work.

TONY TUCKER, IBF 1987

Tony Tucker, born Grand Rapids, Michigan, on 28 December 1958, was shaping up as the best of the Alphabet Boys until he ran into the iron fists of Mike Tyson. He won the IBF title on 30 May 1987, by stopping James 'Buster' Douglas in ten rounds. Three months later he took a pounding from Tyson, but managed to survive the full 12 rounds and was holding his own up until the last third of the exhausting fight.

He went off the rails after his points defeat and got involved in the drugs scene. Tucker shaped up well enough in a comeback campaign to earn a title shot against Lennox Lewis in a WBC championship contest in Las Vegas on 8 May 1993. He climbed off the canvas to give Lewis a tough battle before losing the 12-round decision on points.

In April 1995 he was stopped in seven rounds in a showdown with Bruce Seldon for the vacant WBA title. He later had his licence revoked because of concerns over his vision. Tucker revealed long after his Tyson defeat that he had gone into the fight with a right hand fractured in a sparring session ten days before the contest.

FRANCESCO DAMIANI, WBO 1989–1991

Francesco Damiani, born Kavenna, Italy, on 4 October 1958, had an amateur career, the highlight of which was a victory over triple Olympic champion Teofilo Stevenson. He was the silver medallist at the Los Angeles Olympics in 1984, losing on points to Tyrell Biggs in the final.

After winning the European title as a professional Damiani became the first holder of yet another confusing version of the world heavyweight championship as the title became further devalued. He knocked out South African Johnny Duplooy in three rounds on 6 May 1989 to win the WBO crown. He successfully defended the title against Daniel Netto in 1990 before being knocked out by Ray Mercer in the ninth round in Atlantic City on 11 January 1991. Damiani beat former champion Greg Page in a comeback campaign, but was hammered in the following bout in 1993 by Oliver McCall, ending his career. It was later claimed in a high-profile court case that he had connections with the Mob and that attempts had been made to fix one of his major fights.

RAY MERCER, WBO 1991

Ray Mercer, born Jacksonville, Florida, on 4 April 1961, was a US Army sergeant when he won the 1988 Olympic heavyweight gold medal. He made rapid progress as a professional, and after outpointing Bert Cooper in a war in 1990 he knocked out Francesco Damiani in nine rounds to win the WBO crown.

After blasting out 'White Hope' Tommy Morrison in five rounds, he was stripped of the WBO title for agreeing to a match against the veteran Larry Holmes at Atlantic City on 7 February 1992. He was soundly outpointed and his championship value dropped several points.

Mercer got involved in a bribery scandal when he was alleged to have offered his opponent, Jesse Ferguson, money to lose. He was said to have made the offer during the fight that could have earned him another crack at the title. Ferguson won on points.

He later switched to martial arts combat, and became a spokesman for a project aimed at helping youngsters take the right road in life.

MICHAEL MOORER, WBO 1992; WBA and IBF 1994

Michael Moorer, born Brooklyn, New York, on 12 November 1967, was a product of the Detroit Kronk Gym, and became the first southpaw heavyweight champion of the century when he twice got off the canvas to stop Bert Cooper in the fifth round of a fight for the vacant WBO title on 15 May 1992.

He surrendered the championship to pursue more lucrative prizes and on 22 April 1994 – inspired by Tyson's former trainer Teddy Atlas – he stunned Evander Holyfield by outpointing him over 12 rounds. But before the year was out he had walked into the mighty right hand of George Foreman and was an ex-champion.

Moorer was one of only four men (the others being Muhammad Ali, Evander Holyfield and Lennox Lewis) to win a heavyweight world title on three separate occasions, as well as being one of only four men (the others being Bob Fitzsimmons, Michael Spinks and Roy Jones Jr.) to win world titles at both light-heavyweight and heavyweight.

Since retiring from the ring, Moorer has worked as a boxing trainer alongside Freddie Roach at the Wild Card gym in Los Angeles.

TOMMY MORRISON, WBO 1993

Tommy Morrison, born Gravette, Arizona, on 2 January 1969, was being billed as the new great American 'White Hope' until he was comprehensively beaten by Ray Mercer when challenging for the WBO title in Atlantic City on 18 October 1991. The publicity drums had been beating hard for Morrison, who was related to Hollywood hero John Wayne. He was given a starring role opposite Sylvester Stallone in *Rocky V*, but the script went wrong for him in the real ring when Mercer trapped him on the ropes in the fifth round and knocked him cold with a volley of punches to the jaw.

They picked Morrison up and put him together again and in Las Vegas on 7 June 1993 he had too much stamina and steam for old George Foreman, and outpointed him over 12 laborious rounds.

In his first defence Morrison stopped the obscure Tim Tomashek, who had been brought out of the audience at the last minute when the original opponent pulled out. The WBO later withdrew recognition of the sham of a title fight.

Morrison then put his championship on the line against Michael Bentt in Tulsa on 29 October 1993. Few experts gave Bentt a hope of winning. Morrison clearly thought he had an easy job on his hands and came rushing across the ring in search of a quick knockout and soon had Bentt on the ropes under an all-out attack. He forgot about defence and was wide open as Bentt threw a counterpunch that landed on his suspect jaw and the referee stopped the fight with Morrison floundering and in trouble. It was as if the Indians had upped and massacred John Wayne.

His chances of battling his way back into the title picture disappeared in October 1995 when he was stopped in six one-sided rounds by Lennox Lewis.

Morrison's life went into freefall and he served a prison sentence after various skirmishes on the wrong side of the law. In 1998 he was diagnosed as suffering from HIV, and died of AIDS on 1 September 2013, aged 44.

MICHAEL BENTT, WBO 1993–1994

Michael Bentt, born to Jamaican parents in East Dulwich, London, on 4 September 1965, was raised in the US. After a distinguished amateur career he took one of the quickest routes of all time to a world heavyweight title. He was knocked out in his debut and just 11 fights later was hailed as the WBO champion after his shock victory over Tommy Morrison.

Bentt then came to London to defend the championship against Herbie Hide at Millwall Football Club's ground on 19 March 1994. The publicity hype for the fight got out of control, and both boxers were fined by the British Boxing Board for scrapping in front of photographers in the street. 'A clash of egos' was how the ultra-intelligent Bentt described it.

Hide was always in command in the official fight against Bentt, who seemed listless, weak and unsteady from the opening exchanges. He was taken to hospital after being knocked out in the seventh round and there were brain damage scares. He retired on medical advice and switched his considerable energies to a remarkable new career as an actor, broadcaster, theatre director and acting coach. Among his screen appearances was a starring role as Sonny Liston in the *Ali* film.

HERBIE HIDE, WBO 1994

Herbie Hide, born Amauzuri, Nigeria, on 27 August 1971 and raised in Norfolk, captured the WBO title in his 26th professional fight. He had won all but one of his contests inside the distance. Few of his opponents were of any real quality, and in March 1995 he took an enormous step up in class when putting his title on the line against Riddick Bowe, who was too big and strong for him and knocked him out in the sixth round.

Hide, a flashy boxer with fast fists and thunderous punching power, stopped Conroy Nelson in two rounds in front of his hometown fans in Norwich on 21 January 1992 to win the vacant WBC international title. Just over a year later he added the vacant British championship to his collection when stopping Michael Murray in five rounds at Dagenham.

He relinquished the British crown to concentrate on his world title ambitions, and gave a flawless performance against Michael Bentt, before regaining the now-vacant WBO title in June 1997 by knocking out Tony Tucker in two rounds.

Hide himself was dispatched in two rounds when he put his title up against Vitali Klitschko at the London

Arena in June 1999. He later campaigned as a cruiserweight before getting a 22-month prison sentence after pleading guilty to conspiracy to supply cocaine following a sting operation engineered by Fleet Street's 'Fake Sheikh' Mazher Mahmood.

He later got involved in a dispute over land ownership in Nigeria, and then helped his son launch a professional boxing career. Both Riddick Bowe and Michael Bentt described him as 'the hardest puncher I ever faced'. Herbie was an enigma wrapped in a riddle and few people ever got to be able to read him.

OLIVER McCALL, WBC 1994

Oliver McCall, born in Chicago on 21 April 1965, was more famous as Mike Tyson's sparring partner than a world title contender until he exploded his right fist on the jaw of Lennox Lewis at Wembley Arena on 24 September 1994. Success had come late for McCall. He was approaching 30 when he stopped Lewis, but with five children to feed he was a hungry fighter and ready to take on all comers. Larry Holmes was the next in line for him, with Frank Bruno waiting in the wings. He outpointed Holmes, but then came unstuck in his second defence against Bruno, who had often hired McCall as a sparring partner.

McCall – nicknamed the 'Atomic Bull' – had put together a record of only 29 fights in his nine years, preferring to acrue most of his earning in the gymnasium as a sparring partner for champions and leading contenders.

At 6ft 2in, he conceded three inches in height to Lewis but prepared himself to throw right hand bombs over the sometimes lazy Lewis left lead. His plan worked to perfection, and when he detonated his right it flattened Lewis and stunned the Wembley crowd.

In June 1997 he suffered what was described as 'a mental breakdown' during a return fight with Lewis in Las Vegas for the vacant WBC crown. The referee stopped the contest in the fifth round as McCall wept. He had a tough chin and was never knocked down but he took plenty of head punches against both Lewis and Bruno.

Despite drug-related problems and several arrests and probation sentences, McCall boxed on until 2014, finishing his career against low-ranked opponents in Germany and Poland. He was 53 when he had his last fight in 2018.

FRANK BRUNO, WBC 1995

Frank Bruno, born Hammersmith, London, on 16 November 1961, deserved a special award for perseverance when he won the WBC version of the world heavyweight championship on a memorable night at Wembley Stadium in the late summer of 1995. It was his fourth bid for the title following defeats by Tim Witherspoon (1986), Mike Tyson (1989) and Lennox Lewis (1993).

He became the new WBC champion by outpointing his former sparring partner Oliver McCall over 12 tense rounds. Long before this triumph Bruno had cemented himself into the hearts of the British public with his engaging personality and natural humility. His popularity transcended boxing, and the long-awaited title win made him arguably the most popular sportsman in the land.

Bruno's career was almost over before it had even started. After becoming at 18 the youngest ever ABA heavyweight champion, he was found to be short-sighted in one eye and before he could get a professional licence he had to fly to Colombia for what was then a rare retina operation that cured his problem. His march towards title status was rudely interrupted in his 22nd fight when he was knocked out in the tenth and final round while way ahead on points against James 'Bonecrusher' Smith.

His then manager Terry Lawless patiently steered him to world title fights against Tim Witherspoon and Mike Tyson, both of which he lost after starting in impressive style. Following another eye operation, this time for a torn retina, he got a third crack at the championship and was giving a good account of himself against Lennox Lewis when he walked into a left hook and was stopped in the seventh round.

Ignoring widespread calls for his retirement, fitness fanatic Bruno returned to the gymnasium and adopted a new aggressive approach under the guidance of his trainer George Francis. All his hard work paid off with his victory over McCall, and suddenly this proud father of two daughters and a son was in the driving seat for a mega-money return match with Mike Tyson, when he was stopped in three rounds.

He then hung up his gloves. Since his retirement Frank has come through a personal crisis caused by a bipolar condition, and is now a popular motivational speaker for people with mental health problems.

I was Frank's publicist for ten years from when he was just 18 and I have never known a more dedicated and determined competitor in a lifetime spent around sportsmen. He thoroughly earned his brief reign as a world heavyweight champion. The way he has fought and conquered bipolar problems post-retirement speaks volumes about his strength of character. Nice one, Frank.

BRUCE SELDON, WBA 1995–1996

Bruce Seldon, born New Jersey, on 30 January 1967, was nicknamed the 'Atlantic City Express'. He won the vacant

WBA title in his 35th fight after forcing Tony Tucker to retire on his stool with eye and nose injuries at the end of seven tough rounds in Las Vegas on 8 April 1995.

Four month later, Seldon fought on the undercard of the Mike Tyson–Peter McNeeley fight that marked Tyson's return to boxing after his prison sentence. Making a first defence of his title, Seldon used his powerful left jab to control Joe Hipp and stop him in the tenth round.

Promoter Don King, calling all the shots, then matched Seldon in a second defence against Tyson on 7 September 1996. There were shouts of 'fix' from ringside spectators when Seldon came off the rails, appearing to go down and out in the first round to what were described as phantom punches from Tyson. Seldon made two abortive comebacks and fought on into his 40s before concentrating on training his son Isiah, a highly rated super-middleweight.

FRANCOIS BOTHA, IBF 1995; WBF 2009–2010

Francois Botha, born Witbank, South Africa, on 28 September 1968, was nicknamed the 'White Buffalo' because of his squat yet massive physique. He scored a hotly disputed 12-round points decision over Axel Schulz to take the vacant IBF title in Stuttgart on 9 December 1995. The lumbering South African, unbeaten in 36 fights, was jeered from the ring by angry German fans.

After Botha failed a drugs test, the result of the fight was then changed to a no contest and the IBF did not recognise Botha, although he was introduced as a former champ in every subsequent professional boxing contest.

In 1996 Botha earned plaudits with a courageous effort against Michael Moorer for the IBF crown on the undercard of Mike Tyson's first contest with Evander Holyfield.

Moorer knocked him out in the 12th round. This eventually led to fights with Tyson (a knockout loss in the fifth round), Shannon Briggs (a draw after ten rounds), and heavyweight title showdowns with Lennox Lewis (lost on a stoppage in the second round) and Wladimir Klitschko (lost on a stoppage in the eighth round).

On 6 February 2009, Botha beat Ron 'Rocky' Guerrero by unanimous points decision for the vacant WBF heavyweight title in South Africa.

Veteran Evander Holyfield knocked out Botha in eight rounds to claim the WBF championship in Las Vegas on 10 April 2010.

Sporting a white beard and looking every one of his 45 years, the South African was fed to New Zealand prospect Joseph Parker in Auckland in 2013. Parker powered to victory in two one-sided rounds.

Botha, a born warrior, also dabbled in the martial arts and kickboxing world, and continued to switch between the disciplines into his late 40s.

DEONTAY WILDER, WBC 2015–2020

Deontay Wilder, born Tuscaloosa, Alabama, on 22 October 1985, made ten successful defences of his WBC championship before colliding with Britain's Gypsy King, Tyson Fury. He pumped the pride back into American heavyweight boxing, becoming the first USA-born champion since 2007 when outpointing Canadian Bermane Stiverne on 17 January 2015 to win the WBC title.

Coming late to boxing at the age of 20, he collected a bronze medal at the 2008 Olympics before winning all but one of his first 40 professional fights inside the distance. His knockout-to-win ratio stood at 97.5 per cent, with 19 first-round knockouts. Purists were critical of his tendency to slap when launching his major assaults, but nobody could deny the power of the Bronze Bomber's punches.

He won the title on the 73rd birthday of his idol Muhammad Ali and dedicated the victory to his hero. Then, just as he was being considered unbeatable, along came the extraordinary Tyson Fury to wreck his reputation.

World Heavyweight Title Bouts

1890s

James J. Corbett wko21 John L. Sullivan, New Orleans,
09/07/1892

James J. Corbett wko3 Charlie Mitchell, Jacksonville,
25/01/1894

Bob Fitzsimmons wko14 James J. Corbett, Carson City,
17/03/1897

James J. Jeffries wko11 Bob Fitzsimmons, Coney Island,
09/06/1899

James J. Jeffries wpts25 Tom Sharkey, Coney Island,
03/11/1899

1900s

James J. Jeffries wko23 James J. Corbett, Coney Island,
11/05/1900

James J. Jeffries wret5 Gus Ruhlin, San Francisco,
15/11/1901

James J. Jeffries wko8 Bob Fitzsimmons, San Francisco,
25/07/1902

James J. Jeffries wko10 James J. Corbett, San Francisco, 14/08/1903

James J. Jeffries wko2 Jack Munroe, San Francisco, 26/08/1904 (Jeffries announced his retirement as undefeated champion)

Marvin Hart wrsf12 Jack Root, Reno, 03/07/1905

Tommy Burns wpts20 Marvin Hart, Los Angeles, 23/02/1906

Tommy Burns wko15 Jim Flynn, Los Angeles, 02/10/1906

Tommy Burns d20 Phil Jack O'Brien, Los Angeles, 28/11/1906

Tommy Burns wpts20 Jack O'Brien, Los Angeles, 08/05/1907

Tommy Burns wko1 Bill Squires, California, 04/07/1907

Tommy Burns wko10 Gunner Moir, London, 02/12/1907

Tommy Burns wko4 Jack Palmer, London, 10/02/1908

Tommy Burns wko1 Jem Roche, Dublin, 17/03/1908

Tommy Burns wko5 Jewey Smith, Paris, 18/04/1908

Tommy Burns wko13 Bill Squires, Paris, 13/06/1908

Tommy Burns wko13 Bill Squires, Sydney, 24/08/1908

Tommy Burns wko6 Bill Lang, Melbourne, 02/09/1908

Jack Johnson wrsf14 Tommy Burns, Sydney, 26/12/1908

Jack Johnson wko12 Stanley Ketchel, Colma, 16/10/1909

1910s

Jack Johnson wrsf15 James J. Jeffries, Reno, 04/07/1910

Jack Johnson wrsf9 Jim Flynn, Las Vegas, New Mexico, 04/07/1912

Jack Johnson wko2 Andre Spoul, Paris, 28/11/1913

Jack Johnson drew10 Jim Johnson, Paris, 19/12/1913

Jack Johnson wpts20 Frank Moran, Paris, 27/06/1914

Jess Willard wko26 Jack Johnson, Havana, 05/04/1915

Jess Willard nodec10 Frank Moran, New York, 25/03/1916

Jack Dempsey wret3 Jess Willard, Toledo, 04/07/1919

1920s

Jack Dempsey wko3 Billy Miske, Benton Harbour, 06/09/1920

Jack Dempsey wko12 Bill Brennan, New York, 14/12/1920

Jack Dempsey wko4 Georges Carpentier, Jersey City, 02/07/1921

Jack Dempsey wpts15 Tom Gibbons, Montana, 04/07/1923

Jack Dempsey wko2 Luis Ángel Firpo, New York, 14/09/1923

Gene Tunney wpts10 Jack Dempsey, Philadelphia, 23/09/1926

Gene Tunney wpts10 Jack Dempsey, Chicago, 22/09/1927

Gene Tunney wrsf11 Tom Heeney, New York, 23/07/1928 (Tunney announced his retirement as undefeated champion)

1930s

Max Schmeling wdis4 Jack Sharkey, New York, 12/06/1930

Max Schmeling wrsf15 Young Stribling, Cleveland, 03/07/1931

Jack Sharkey wpts15 Max Schmeling, Long Island, 21/06/1932

Primo Carnera wko6 Jack Sharkey, Long Island, 29/06/1933

Primo Carnera wpts15 Paulino Uzcudun, Rome, 22/10/1933

Primo Carnera wpts15 Tommy Loughran, Miami,
01/03/1934

Max Baer wrsf11 Primo Carnera, Long Island,
14/06/1934

James J. Braddock wpts15 Max Baer, Long Island,
13/06/1935

Joe Louis wko8 James J. Braddock, Chicago, 22/06/1937

Joe Louis wpts15 Tommy Farr, New York, 30/08/1937

Joe Louis wko3 Nathan Mann, New York, 23/02/1938

Joe Louis wko5 Harry Thomas, Chicago, 01/04/1938

Joe Louis wko1 Max Schmeling, New York, 22/06/1938

Joe Louis wrsf1 John Henry Lewis, New York,
25/01/1939

Joe Louis wko1 Jack Roper, Los Angeles, 17/04/1939

Joe Louis wrsf4 Tony Galento, New York, 28/06/1939

Joe Louis wko11 Bob Pastor, Detroit, 20/09/1939

1940s

Joe Louis wpts15 Arturo Godoy, New York, 09/02/1940

Joe Louis wrsf2 Johnny Paychek, New York, 29/03/1940

Joe Louis wrsf8 Arturo Godoy, New York, 20/06/1940

Joe Louis wret6 Al McCoy, Boston, 16/12/1940

Joe Louis wko5 Red Burman, New York, 31/01/1941

Joe Louis wko2 Gus Dorazio, Philadelphia, 17/02/1941

Joe Louis wrsf13 Abe Simon, Detroit, 21/03/1941

Joe Louis wrsf9 Tony Musto, St Louis, 08/04/1941

Joe Louis wdis7 Buddy Baer, Washington, 23/05/1941

Joe Louis wko13 Billy Conn, New York, 18/06/1941

Joe Louis wrsf6 Lou Nova, New York, 28/09/1941

Joe Louis wko1 Buddy Baer, New York, 09/01/1942

Joe Louis wko6 Abe Simon, New York, 27/03/1942

Joe Louis wko8 Billy Conn, New York, 19/06/1946

Joe Louis wko1 Tami Mauriello, New York, 18/09/1946

Joe Louis wpts15 Jersey Joe Walcott, New York,
05/12/1947

Joe Lous wko11 Jersey Joe Walcott, New York,
25/06/1948 (Louis announced his retirement as
undefeated champion)

Ezzard Charles wpts15 Jersey Joe Walcott, Chicago,
22/06/1949 (NBA title)

Ezzard Charles wrsf7 Gus Lesnevich, New York,
10/08/1949

Ezzard Charles wko8 Pat Valentino, San Francisco,
14/10/1949

1950s

Ezzard Charles wrsf14 Freddy Beshore, Buffalo,
15/08/1950

Ezzard Charles wpts15 Joe Louis, New York, 27/09/1950
(undisputed title)

Ezzard Charles wko11 Nick Barone, Cincinnati,
05/12/1950

Ezzard Charles wrsf10 Lee Oma, New York, 12/01/1951

Ezzard Charles wpts15 Jersey Joe Walcott, Detroit,
07/03/1951

Ezzard Charles wpts15 Joey Maxim, Chicago, 30/05/1951

Jersey Joe Walcott wko7 Ezzard Charles, Pittsburgh,
18/07/1951

Jersey Joe Walcott wpts15 Ezzard Charles, Philadelphia,
05/06/1952

Rocky Marciano wko13 Jersey Joe Walcott, Philadelphia,
23/09/1952

Rocky Marciano wko1 Jersey Joe Walcott, Chicago,
15/05/1953

Rocky Marciano wrsf11 Roland LaStarza, New York,
24/09/1953

Rocky Marciano wpts15 Ezzard Charles, New York,
17/06/1954

Rocky Marciano wko8 Ezzard Charles, New York,
17/09/1954

Rocky Marciano wrsf9 Don Cockell, San Francisco,
16/05/1955

Rocky Marciano wko9 Archie Moore, New York,
21/09/1955 (Marciano announced his retirement as
undefeated champion)

Floyd Patterson wko5 Archie Moore, Chicago,
30/11/1956

Floyd Patterson wrsf10 Tommy Jackson, New York,
29/07/1957

Floyd Patterson wko6 Pete Rademacher, Seattle,
22/08/1957

Floyd Patterson wret12 Roy Harris, Los Angeles,
18/08/1958

Floyd Patterson wko11 Brian London, Indianapolis,
01/05/1959

Ingemar Johansson wrsf3 Floyd Patterson, New York,
26/06/1959

1960s

Floyd Patterson wko5 Ingemar Johansson, New York,
20/06/1960

Floyd Patterson wko6 Ingemar Johansson, Miami,
13/03/1961

Floyd Patterson wko4 Tom McNeeley, Toronto,
04/12/1961

Sonny Liston wko1 Floyd Patterson, Chicago, 25/09/1962

Sonny Liston wko1 Floyd Patterson, Las Vegas, 22/07/1963

Cassius Clay wret6 Sonny Liston, Miami, 25/02/1964
(Clay changed his name to Muhammad Ali. He was

stripped of WBA title because he signed for return
bout with Liston on 14/09/1964)

Ernie Terrell wpts15 Eddie Machen, Chicago,
05/03/1965 (vacant WBA title)

Muhammad Ali wko1 Sonny Liston, Maine, 25/05/1965

Ernie Terrell wpts15 George Chuvalo, Toronto
01/11/1965 (WBA title)

Muhammad Ali wrsf12 Floyd Patterson, Las Vegas,
22/11/1965

Muhammad Ali wpts15 George Chuvalo, Toronto,
29/03/1966

Muhammad Ali wrsf6 Henry Cooper, London, 21/05/1966

Ernie Terrell wpts15 Doug Jones, Houston, 28/06/1966
(WBA title)

Muhammad Ali wko3 Brian London, London,
06/08/1966

Muhammad Ali wrsf12 Karl Mildenberger, Frankfurt,
10/09/1966

Muhammad Ali wrsf3 Cleveland Williams, Houston,
14/11/1966

Muhammad Ali wpts15 Ernie Terrell, Houston,
06/02/1967 (undisputed title)

Muhammad Ali wko7 Zora Folley, New York,
22/03/1967 (Ali stripped of both titles for refusing to
join US Army, 28/04/1967)

Joe Frazier wrsf11 Buster Mathis, New York, 04/03/1968
(New York state version of vacant title)

Jimmy Ellis wpts15 Jerry Quarry, Oakland, 27/04/1968
(WBA version of vacant title)

Joe Frazier wret2 Manuel Ramos, New York, 24/06/1968
(New York state title)

Jimmy Ellis wpts15 Floyd Patterson, Stockholm,
14/09/1968 (WBA title)

Joe Frazier wpts15 Oscar Bonavena, Philadelphia,
    10/12/1968 (New York State title)
Joe Frazier wko1 Dave Zyglewicz, Houston, 22/04/1969
    (New York State title)
Joe Frazier wrsf7 Jerry Quarry, New York, 26/06/1969
    (New York State title)

1970s

Joe Frazier wret4 Jimmy Ellis, New York, 16/02/1970
    (undisputed title)
Joe Frazier wko2 Bob Foster, Detroit, 18/11/1970
Joe Frazier wpts15 Muhammad Ali, New York,
    08/03/1971
Joe Frazier wrsf4 Terry Daniels, New Orleans, 15/01/1972
Joe Frazier wrsf4 Ron Stander, Omaha, 25/05/1972
George Foreman wrsf2 Joe Frazier, Kingston, 22/01/1973
George Foreman wko1 Joe Roman, Tokyo, 01/09/1973
George Foreman wrsf2 Ken Norton, Caracas, 26/03/1974
Muhammad Ali wko8 George Foreman, Kinshasa,
    30/10/1974
Muhammad Ali wrsf15 Chuck Wepner, Cleveland,
    24/03/1975
Muhammad Ali wrsf11 Ron Lyle, Las Vegas, 16/05/1975
Muhammad Ali wpts15 Joe Bugner, Kuala Lumpur,
    01/07/1975
Muhammad Ali wret14 Joe Frazier, Manila, 01/10/1975
Muhammad Ali wko5 Jean-Pierre Coopman, Puerto
    Rico, 10/02/1976
Muhammad Ali wpts15 Jimmy Young, Maryland,
    30/04/1976
Muhammad Ali wrsf5 Richard Dunn, Munich, 25/05/1976
Muhammad Ali wpts15 Ken Norton, New York,
    28/09/1976

Muhammad Ali wpts15 Alfredo Evangelista, Maryland, 16/05/1977

Muhammad Ali wpts15 Earnie Shavers, New York, 29/09/1977

Leon Spinks wpts15 Muhammad Ali, Las Vegas, 15/02/1978 (Spinks was stripped of the WBC version for failure to defend against Ken Norton, who was proclaimed WBC champion)

Larry Holmes wpts15 Ken Norton, Las Vegas, 10/06/1978 (WBC title)

Muhammad Ali wpts15 Leon Spinks, New Orleans, 15/09/1978 (WBA title)

Larry Holmes wko7 Alfredo Evangelista, Las Vegas, 10/11/1978 (WBC title)

Larry Holmes wrsf7 Osvaldo Ocasio, Las Vegas, 24/03/1979

Larry Holmes wrsf12 Mike Weaver, New York, 22/06/1979

Larry Holmes wrsf11 Earnie Shavers, Las Vegas, 28/09/1979 (Ali announced his retirement as WBA champion, September 1979)

John Tate wpts15 Gerrie Coetzee, Johannesburg 20/10/1979 (vacant WBA title)

1980s

Larry Holmes wko6 Lorenzo Zanon, Las Vegas, 03/02/1980

Larry Holmes wrsf8 Leroy Jones, Las Vegas, 31/03/1980

Mike Weaver wko15 John Tate, Knoxville, 31/03/1980 (WBA title)

Larry Holmes wrsf7 Scott Le Doux, Bloomington, 07/07/1980

Larry Holmes wret10 Muhammad Ali, Las Vegas, 02/10/1980

Mike Weaver wko13 Gerrie Coetzee, Sun City,
   25/10/1980 (WBA title)

Larry Holmes wpts15 Trevor Berbick, Las Vegas,
   14/04/1981

Larry Holmes wrsf3 Leon Spinks, Detroit, 12/06/1981

Mike Weaver wpts15 James Tillis, Rosemount,
   03/10/1981 (WBA title)

Larry Holmes wrsf11 Renaldo Snipes, Pittsburgh,
   06/11/1981

Larry Holmes wdis13 Gerry Cooney, Las Vegas, 11/06/1982

Larry Holmes wpts15 Randy Cobb, Houston, 26/11/1982

Michael Dokes wrsf1 Mike Weaver, Las Vegas,
   10/12/1982 (WBA title)

Larry Holmes wpts12 Lucien Rodriguez, Scranton,
   27/03/1983

Larry Holmes wpts12 Tim Witherspoon, Las Vegas,
   20/05/1983

Michael Dokes drew15 Mike Weaver, Las Vegas,
   20/05/1983 (WBA title)

Larry Holmes wrsf5 Scott Frank, Atlantic City,
   10/09/1983

Gerrie Coetzee wko10 Michael Dokes, Richfield,
   23/09/1983 (WBA title; Holmes relinquished WBC
   title and accepted recognition by the newly formed
   International Boxing Federation)

Tim Witherspoon wpts12 Greg Page, Las Vegas,
   09/03/1984 (vacant WBC title)

Pinklon Thomas wpts12 Tim Witherspoon, Las Vegas,
   31/08/1984 (WBC title)

Larry Holmes wrsf12 James Smith, Las Vegas,
   09/11/1984 (IBF title)

Greg Page wko8 Gerrie Coetzee, Sun City, 01/12/1984
   (WBA title)

Larry Holmes wrsf10 David Bey, Las Vegas, 15/03/1985
(IBF title)

Tony Tubbs wpts15 Greg Page, Buffalo, 29/04/1985
(WBA title)

Larry Holmes wpts15 Carl Williams, Reno, 20/05/1985
(IBF title)

Pinklon Thomas wko8 Mike Weaver, Las Vegas,
15/06/1985 (WBC title)

Michael Spinks wpts15 Larry Holmes, Las Vegas,
21/09/1985 (IBF title)

Tim Witherspoon wpts15 Tony Tubbs, Atlanta,
17/01/1986 (WBA title)

Trevor Berbick wpts12 Pinklon Thomas, Las Vegas,
22/03/1986 (WBC title)

Michael Spinks wpts15 Larry Holmes, Las Vegas,
19/04/1986 (IBF title)

Tim Witherspoon wrsf11 Frank Bruno, London,
19/07/1986 (WBA title)

Michael Spinks wrsf4 Steffen Tangstad, Las Vegas,
06/09/1986 (IBF title; Spinks relinquished IBF title,
refusing to defend against Tony Tucker)

Mike Tyson wrsf2 Trevor Berbick, Las Vegas, 22/11/1986
(WBC title)

James Smith wrsf1 Tim Witherspoon, New York,
12/12/1986 (WBA title)

Mike Tyson wpts12 James Smith, Las Vegas, 07/03/1987
(WBA/WBC titles)

Mike Tyson wrsf6 Pinklon Thomas, Las Vegas,
30/05/1987 (WBA/WBC titles)

Tony Tucker wrsf10 James Douglas, Las Vegas,
30/05/1987 (vacant IBF title)

Mike Tyson wpts12 Tony Tucker, Las Vegas, 01/08/1987
(undisputed title)

Mike Tyson wrsf7 Tyrell Biggs, Atlantic City,
   16/10/1987
Mike Tyson wrsf4 Larry Holmes, Atlantic City,
   22/01/1988
Mike Tyson wrsf2 Tony Tubbs, Tokyo, 21/03/1988
Mike Tyson wko1 Michael Spinks, Atlantic City,
   27/06/1988
Mike Tyson wrsf5 Frank Bruno, Las Vegas, 25/02/1989
Francesco Damiani wko3 Johnny Duplooy, Syracuse,
   06/05/1989 (vacant WBO title)
Mike Tyson wrsf1 Carl Williams, Atlantic City,
   31/07/1989
Francesco Damiani wrtd2 Daniel Netto, Cesena,
   16/12/1989 (WBO title)

1990s

James Douglas wko10 Mike Tyson, Tokyo, 11/02/1990
Evander Holyfield wko3 James Douglas, Las Vegas,
   25/10/1990
Ray Mercer wko9 Francesco Damiani, Atlantic City,
   11/01/1991 (WBO title)
Evander Holyfield wpts12 George Foreman, Atlantic
   City, 09/04/1991
Ray Mercer wrsf5 Tommy Morrison, Atlantic City,
   18/10/1991 (WBO title; Mercer was stripped of the
   WBO title because he signed to fight Larry Holmes,
   07/02/1992. Holmes won on points)
Evander Holyfield wrsf7 Bert Cooper, Atlanta,
   23/11/1991
Michael Moorer wrsf5 Bert Cooper, Atlantic City,
   15/05/1992 (vacant WBO title)
Evander Holyfield wpts12 Larry Holmes, Las Vegas,
   19/06/1992

Riddick Bowe wpts12 Evander Holyfield, Las Vegas, 13/11/1992 (Bowe relinquished WBC title after refusing to defend against Lennox Lewis who was named WBC champion on the basis of his second-round stoppage of Donovan 'Razor' Ruddock in London, 31/10/1992)

Riddick Bowe wrsf1 Michael Dokes, New York, 06/02/1993 (WBA/IBF titles)

Lennox Lewis wpts12 Tony Tucker, Las Vegas, 08/05/1993 (WBC title)

Riddick Bowe wrsf2 Jesse Ferguson, Washington, 22/05/1993 (WBA/IBF titles; Moorer relinquished WBO title to pursue other belts)

Tommy Morrison wpts12 George Foreman, Las Vegas, 07/06/1993 (vacant WBO title)

Tommy Morrison wrsf4 Tim Tomashek, Kansas City, 30/08/1993 (WBO title; the WBO later rescinded the decision to sanction the fight because of Tomashek's lack of experience)

Lennox Lewis wrsf7 Frank Bruno, Cardiff, 01/10/1993 (WBC title)

Michael Bentt wrsf1 Tommy Morrison, Tulsa, 29/10/1993 (WBO title)

Evander Holyfield wpts12 Riddick Bowe, Las Vegas, 06/11/1993 (WBA/IBF titles)

Herbie Hide wko7 Michael Bentt, London, 19/03/1994 (WBO title)

Michael Moorer wpts12 Evander Holyfield, Las Vegas, 22/04/1994 (WBA/IBF titles)

Lennox Lewis wrsf8 Phil Jackson, Atlantic City, 06/05/1994 (WBC title)

Oliver McCall wrsf2 Lennox Lewis, London, 24/09/1994 (WBC title)

George Foreman wko10 Michael Moorer, Las Vegas, 05/11/1994 (WBA/IBF titles; Foreman stripped of the WBA title for agreeing to defend against the unrated German Axel Schulz. Tony Tucker and Bruce Seldon nominated to fight for the vacant title)

Riddick Bowe wko6 Herbie Hide, Las Vegas, 11/03/1995 (WBO title)

Bruce Seldon wrtd7 Tony Tucker, Las Vegas, 08/04/1995 (WBA title)

Oliver McCall wpts12 Larry Holmes, Las Vegas, 08/04/1995 (WBC title)

George Foreman wpts12 Axel Schulz, Las Vegas, 22/04/1995 (IBF title)

Riddick Bowe wko6 Jorge González, Las Vegas, 17/06/1995 (WBO title; Bowe stopped Evander Holyfield in eight rounds in a non-title fight in Las Vegas on 4 November 1995. Foreman stripped of IBF title)

Frank Bruno wpts12 Oliver McCall, London, 02/09/1995 (WBC title)

Francois Botha wpts12 Axel Schulz, Stuttgart, 09/12/1995 (IBF title)

Since the mid-1990s, the proliferation of titles has become ridiculous, diluting the lineal championship. You will see what we mean as you study this list of the claimants since 2000, not including Lennox Lewis, the Klitschko brothers and most of the champions featured in the Alphabet Boys section:

Chris Byrd (United States) WBO 2000; IBF 2002–2006
John Ruiz (United States) WBA 2001–2003; 2004–2005
Roy Jones Jr. (United States) WBA 2003–2004
Corrie Sanders (South Africa) WBO 2003
Lamon Brewster (United States) WBO 2004–2006
Nikolai Valuev (Russia) WBA 2005–2007; 2008–2009
Sergei Liakhovich (Belarus) WBO 2006
Oleg Maskaev (Russia) WBC 2006–2008
Ruslan Chagaev (Uzbekistan) WBA 2007–2009; 2014–
    2016; 2016
Sultan Ibragimov (Russia) WBO 2007–2008
Samuel Peter (Nigeria) WBC 2008
David Haye (United Kingdom) WBA 2009–2011
Alexander Povetkin (Russia) WBA 2011–2013
Bermane Stiverne (Canada) WBC 2014–2015
Deontay Wilder (United States) WBC 2015–2021
Tyson Fury (United Kingdom) IBF, WBA Super and
    WBO 2015, then in 2021 and 2022 claiming to be the
    lineal champion after beating Deontay Wilder
Charles Martin (United States) IBF 2016
Lucas Browne (Australia) WBA 2016
Joseph Parker (New Zealand) WBO 2016–2017
Manuel Charr (Germany/Lebanon) WBA 2017–2021
Anthony Joshua (United Kingdom) IBF 2016, WBA
    Super, WBO, IBO 2017, WBO 2018 (lost his titles to

Oleksandr Usyk after regaining them from Andy Ruiz
Jr. in December 2019, following June 2019 defeat
Oleksandr Usyk (Ukraine) WBA, WBO and IBF 2021–

This is a table in progress, but what is generally accepted
by all good judges is that THE heavyweight king going
into 2023 was the self-styled Gypsy King, Tyson Fury.

And Oleksandr Osyk was waiting to dispute Fury's
claim to be world champion.

The world heavyweight roundabout continues to roll.

Keep punching …